THE HERITAGE OF LONGWOOD

THE HERITAGE OF LONGWOOD

William L. Whitwell

UNIVERSITY PRESS OF MISSISSIPPI
Jackson

Copyright © 1975 by the
University Press of Mississippi
Library of Congress Catalog Card Number 74-17510
ISBN: -1-60473-398-5
Manufactured in the United States of America

Print-on-Demand Edition

Dedicated

to

Don M. Dunifon

who inspired the quest

and to

Mr. and Mrs. William Carl McGehee

and

Alma Carpenter

who made it possible

Contents

Acknowledgments ix
Chapter 1 Longwood: A New Idea 3
Chapter 2 The People of Longwood 19
Chapter 3 The Octagon Concept 29
Chapter 4 The Construction of Longwood 43
Chapter 5 The Furnishings of Longwood 59
Chapter 6 War and Aftermath 69
Chapter 7 Twentieth-Century Longwood 83
Appendix: Specifications 97
Bibliography 103
Index 107

Acknowledgments

Many people have contributed their time and effort in the preparation of this work. Mrs. Margaret Shields Hendrix offered encouragement and comment from the beginning. Dr. Thomas Howard Gandy and his son, Tom, helped tremendously with photographs. The Natchez Pilgrimage Garden Club kindly assisted throughout, as did Mr. and Mrs. Anthony Burns, current custodians of Longwood, and Mr. Dix Fowler, whose work on the restoration has been so important.

The generosity of Hollins College in allotting Ford Foundation and Mellon Foundation funds made a great deal of this research possible.

Professor Frances Niederer and librarians Mrs. Charles Mitchell and Miss Shirley Henn took time from busy schedules to help, while the typing skills of Mrs. T. L. Griffith were invaluable. The Honorable M. Caldwell Butler, U.S. House of Representatives, made a trip to Washington a pleasure.

Thanks are also due Miss Laura Carpenter, whose photographs have created an unparalleled record of Longwood today, and Mrs. Kelly McAdams, whose privately printed book, *The Building of Longwood,* has been invaluable in this research. Reprinting much Sloan-Nutt correspondence and many specifications, the McAdams book makes much documentation of Longwood clear.

THE HERITAGE OF LONGWOOD

FIGURE 1. Samuel Sloan's proposal for "An Oriental Villa," Design 49 in his book *The Model Architect* of 1852. This was the inspiration for Longwood.

Chapter 1

Longwood: A New Idea

One day in April, 1861, at the construction site of Longwood Villa near Natchez, Mississippi, work was abruptly halted. Tools were dropped with a clatter as the builders fled the area, leaving their monumental task unfinished. Civil War was rolling over the South. Disruption, unrest, and fear had all combined to drive Dr. Nutt's skilled artisans away from Mississippi, back to their homes in Philadelphia. They had to go quickly, while time remained, while transportation back to Pennsylvania was still available. Local workmen also joined the exodus from Longwood's spacious grounds, and hurried to rally to the Confederate cause.

Longwood Villa today stands essentially as it was left in 1861, the tools dropped by the frightened workers still lying where they fell. The place, an unfulfilled dream, is an architectural curiosity in an overgrown setting two miles from downtown Natchez.

In the second half of the nineteenth century, the architecture of grand homes of the southern plantation country had reached a saturation point in Greek Revival style. In the North, architectural progression had created a vacuum into which Gothic Revival and Eclectic styles had moved. Taste-makers were decreeing that any style would now do; visual effect was all that counted. Dr. Haller Nutt, looking for an opportunity both to accommodate the taste arbiters and to indulge an urge to innovate, had therefore set out in the late 1850s toward his goal of erecting a truly different style of home. An aristocratic cotton planter in his mid-forties, Dr. Nutt was also a physician and scientist. Wealthy and cultured, he was building what he considered a modern mansion on broad acreage high above the Mississippi River.

Nutt's vision began with his perusal of *The Model Architect,* Samuel Sloan's book of house designs published in 1852. The forty-ninth design was "An Oriental Villa" (Figure 1). Sloan wrote that this particular style of architecture was not widely known in the United States and had not been adopted for any public buildings and for only a few residences. He noted that such a villa should be of generous size. Sloan felt the building would need ornaments "to render it pleasing," though ornamentation would increase the expense without adding to the "comfort or convenience of the edifice." Nutt's imagination must have been stimulated as he read: "There are, however, some cases where these objections are of little force; and many persons, contemplating building, seek for a design, at once original, striking, appropriate and picturesque."[1]

Sloan continued with a lengthy description of the origins of the style going from the "Arabians" via the Gothic to Spain, "Cordova and the Alhambra as described by Irving," and thence to Sta. Sophia, "that venerable pile." He described the exterior design as "sufficiently modest for a private dwelling, yet striking in conception, and bold in outline." Sloan added that the whole should be capped by a "Persian dome" and flanked by minarets. The latter features were not, however, included on the subsequent Longwood plans.

Two plates in Sloan's book (Figures 2 and 3) showed the floor plans and introduced the room arrangements but offered no comment other than giving the functions of each chamber. The vertical section (Figure 4), however, did give an idea of the magnificence Sloan foresaw for the building. Showing the "end of the vestibule, parlor and hall on the first floor, and, on the second the gallery and entrance doors to the chambers," the drawing vividly indicated splendors Nutt could anticipate. Concerning the domed interior Sloan noted, "We would recommend painting in frescoe *(sic),* as being at once both chaste and economical." He continued, "By the exercise

Longwood: A New Idea

of skill and good taste, the most pleasing and striking effects may be produced at modest expense." The next two plates showed details of the decorations planned for the windows of the verandas (Figures 5 and 6). These were more ornate, but similar to the ones later designed for Longwood. Description of the proposed "Oriental Villa" ended with a "bill of items for the house which includes materials as well as some labor —$27,868.00 at the prices of labor and materials prevailing near this city" (Philadelphia). Sloan's designs for the villa were to be the inspiration on which Haller Nutt would build his dream house.[2]

As the walls of Longwood Villa rose on the structure's octagonal foundation in accordance with the plans of architect Samuel Sloan, and as the elaborate trimmings were set in place, the building became a source of much speculation. Debate centered on the question of what its style really was. All observers agreed that it was oriental in concept, but descriptions ranged from Oriental Revival to Moslem Revival, to Moorish–Byzantine and Persian.

One 1863 traveler to Natchez, carrying a letter of introduction to Dr. Nutt from a mutual acquaintance, wrote of his visit:

> ... Natchez is a pretty little town, and ought to contain about 6,000 inhabitants. It is built on the top of a high bluff overlooking the Mississippi River, which is about three quarters of a mile broad at this point.
>
> When I reached Natchez I hired a carriage, and, with a letter of introduction which I had brought from San Antonio, I drove to the house of Mr. Haller Nutt, distant from the town about two miles.
>
> The scenery about Natchez is extremely pretty and the ground is hilly, with plenty of fine trees. Mr. Nutt's place reminded me very much of an English gentleman's country seat, except that the house itself is rather like a pagoda, but it is beautifully furnished.[3]

Furnishings could, of course, only have been on the ground floor then.

The interior seems to have occasioned additional debate.

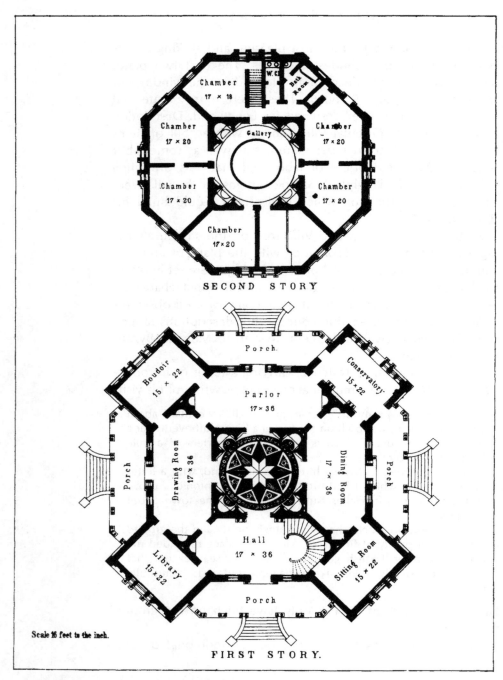

FIGURE 2. Novel utilization of walls within the octagon form combined with the large rooms was to create much open space on the first story.

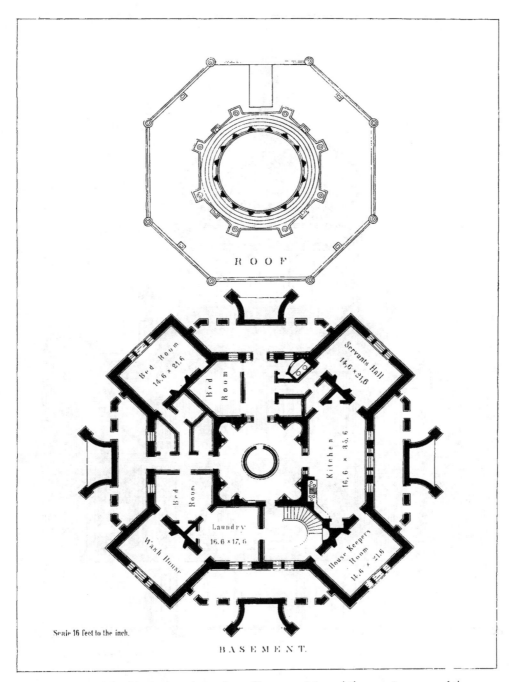

FIGURE 3. The basement plan shows how Sloan envisioned the service area of the house. The Nutt family would live in this area when the Civil War broke out.

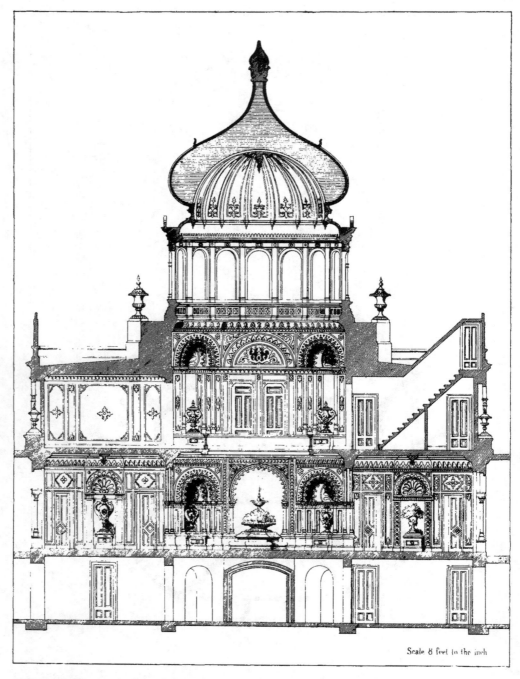

FIGURE 4. The vertical section of the proposed house shows the magnificence Samuel Sloan forsaw for the interior. Decoration would have been in the manner he suggested here.

FIGURE 5. Detail of the proposed window decoration from Sloan's *Model Architect* of 1852. The Moorish arches are similar to those used later on Longwood.

FIGURE 6. Decoration detail from the "Oriental Villa" design in Sloan's *Model Architect* shows luxurious carved decoration which could be applied to the octagon structure.

Longwood: A New Idea

In *Natchez on the Mississippi,* author Harnett Kane notes that the inside of the new Longwood was more puzzling than the exterior.

> On every floor was to be a central eight-sided room, with eight doors leading to eight outer sections. Each room had eight panels, downstairs the first object of furniture would be an eight-sided settee. Not a hallway could be found; whether this was something Moorish or Arabesque, or merely Nutt, is not clear. As the family explained, you would be able to walk around the house from any direction, "without opening the same door twice" . . . The inventive Haller was planning in 1860 a system of indirect lighting with mirrors. He installed large ones in the dome and arranged glassed-over openings on each floor. On bright days every one of the thirty rooms would have sunlight.[4]

The sixteen-sided clerestory would admit light from above. The edifice was topped with a huge dome, often characterized as Byzantine–Moorish.

The great Moorish-Byzantine dome on top of Longwood has fascinated visitors to Natchez ever since 1861. Sixteen clerestory windows, blocked up today, were to admit light into the center rotunda.

THE HERITAGE OF LONGWOOD

Samuel Sloan did not originate the octagonal house, but he ranked among the leaders of a minor movement to refine the concept behind it and make it practical. At the time Longwood was under construction, many octagonal homes had already been built from Maine to California. In New York state alone, 126 such houses were reportedly completed and in use. The man who popularized the octagonal dwelling was Orson Squire Fowler, who later lived in one of his own creations in Fishkill, New York.[5] (It was razed in 1897.) Eccentric Mr. Fowler was a phrenologist, and to architecture no more than a theorist. It was he who advanced the hypothesis later espoused by Sloan, that eight walls enclosed more space and offered more usable room than four walls of equivalent length.[6]

Haller Nutt and his wife Julia seem to have sought out Sloan during one of their trips north to visit their daughters, who attended Madame Chegary's and d'Hervilly's Boarding and Day School for Young Ladies in Philadelphia from 1858 to 1860. Samuel Sloan must have been impressed by the plantation owner's grand ways. Money flowed freely as attested to by the collection of bills and receipts still preserved in the Haller Nutt Collection in Duke University's Perkins Library. A bill from Caldwell, the famous Philadelphia jeweler, indicates that Nutt spent $2,397.75 for "one fine single stone diamond ring" and a number of other items listed as "pearls, mounting, etc." There are also bills for thousands of dollars worth of clothes for Mrs. Nutt and her daughters from stores in Philadelphia and New York.

In that summer of 1859, the family also took a trip into the northeastern United States and Canada. They spent five days at the United States Hotel in Saratoga Springs, New York, and then went on to Montreal's Donegana Hotel, where on August 19 Mr. Nutt signed the register as "self, family, and servant." They were in Quebec for two days, returning to Montreal on August 24 and to Saratoga Springs on the 29th for four days. Next they went to the William Henry Hotel on Lake George for a day, and thence to New York City to stay at the St. Nicholas Hotel. September 6 found them registered at the City

Longwood: A New Idea

Hotel in Baltimore. From there they went back to Philadelphia so the girls could return to school. For the trip home, Mr. and Mrs. Nutt purchased from Andrews and Son a number of trunks, some of which can still be found in dusty corners of the unfinished rooms at Longwood. The Nutts returned to Natchez, via Cincinnati, by Christmas. The new house plans must have occupied much of their winter as the Nutts researched their project.

Sloan designs, including the octagonal residence, appeared frequently in *Godey's Lady's Book,* the most widely read monthly magazine in the country. The *Lady's Book* homes made architecture subject to current fashions. Middle-class ladies of the nineteenth century, just coming into their own culturally, took to the subject avidly. "To keep his readers interested, Godey and his architects were forced, like all arbiters of fashion, into experimentalism." Between 1846 and 1892, the magazine published approximately 450 house designs; for a number of years many of them were Sloan's. Godey, who prided himself in printing only original works, reported more than 4,000 cottages and villas were built from the magazine's published plans. [8]

Many new designs were supplied Godey by Samuel Sloan. The distinguished architect was president of the Philadelphia Chapter of the American Institute of Architects and founder of the *Architectural Review and American Builder's Journal* (1868–70), "which seems to have consisted almost entirely of his own writings." [9] Along with numerous domestic commissions, Sloan designed banks and other public structures. Later in life, he moved to the South, where he designed the Governor's Mansion in Raleigh, North Carolina, among other buildings. In 1876, his designs won second place in the contest for the Philadelphia Exhibition buildings. His career as *Lady's Book* architect in residence was eventually terminated when another architect gained favor. Famed though he was, relatively little is now known about Samuel Sloan, documentation of his life and work having been "hindered by the almost complete lack of any Sloan papers—personal or professional." [10]

THE HERITAGE OF LONGWOOD

A cordial relationship of mutual understanding, admiration, and respect seems to have grown between Nutt and Sloan after their meeting. Correspondence between the two men in 1860 and 1861 reveals that at no time was there friction regarding either points of view or personality, even though Dr. Nutt suggested many changes in Sloan's designs. Nutt frequently deferred to his wife's wishes rather than his own, his letters to the architect often indicating that he had been "outvoted." Afterward, knowing he would receive perfect understanding, the Mississippian might add that he knew the designer would recognize the advisability of making such concessions. In a letter from Winter Quarters (a plantation of Nutt's in Tensas Parish, Louisiana) dated February 3, 1860, the planter–physician set forth a series of suggestions and objections regarding the building plans already developed. Though he presented his own point of view firmly throughout the long and detailed letter, midway in the message Nutt wrote, "I am fearful there is (sic) other points not well agreed upon. [However], in regard to architectural proportions and style of work throughout I feel sure that your taste is far better than Mrs. Nutts (sic) and my own." [11]

In another letter, sent five days later, Dr. Nutt again deferred to the architect's experience and knowledge, stating: "Now you have my suggestions on these different points and all I have to say is to use your own discretion and go ahead." [12] He also noted that it was his aim to be always in advance of the architect—to facilitate matters as much as possible. Throughout the substantial correspondence of February, 1860, Dr. Nutt emphasized that Sloan should follow his own plans. For his part, Sloan valued the good breeding and education of his client as well as Dr. Nutt's taste and personal concepts of quality. The architect must have admired the planter's habit of placing confidence in professional competence and having respect for innovation.

In 1861, long after the client–architect relationship had been initiated, Sloan published his *Sloan's Homestead Architecture*. One passage, in a chapter on style, states:

Longwood today is being carefully preserved by the Pilgrimage Garden Club of Natchez.

Without condemning what has been done, and with great hopes for the future of rural building, we pass sentence on servile imitation as being unworthy of the genius and spirit of the American people. There is an element of originality in American enterprise that seems to have slumbered in nothing more than in the pursuit of architecture as a fine art, and once fully awakened to the importance of its cultivation, it is destined to set its mark high in the record of nations. But this can only be done by the application of the best talent the country can afford, irrespective of the profits likely to accrue to the leaders of the profession. So long as the uneducated builder is permitted to take the lead in designing and constructing our edifices, to the exclusion of the true architect, so long must we fall short of the high standard within our reach.[13]

The passage throws a sidelight on the Sloan–Nutt relationship. Dr. Nutt was not a slavish follower; he was himself an innovator. Sloan could respect that characteristic in his employer even while he believed that a certain amount of deference was the expert's just due. That the relationship between the two men developed so richly indicated that they had much in common intellectually.

In all, about forty-five letters concerning Longwood passed between Sloan and Dr. Nutt in the period 1860-61. The architect's communications usually arrived on his business letterhead. Sloan's stationery gave not only his address, 152 South Fourth Street, Philadelphia, but listed three of his writings on architecture as well—"*Sloan's City and Suburban Architecture* containing numerous Designs and Details for Public and Private Edifices and Mercantile Buildings. Illustrated by 136 Engravings" came first, then "*Sloan's Constructive Architecture,* A Guide to the Practical Builder and Mechanic, containing Designs for Domes, Roofs, Spires, and Examples of the Five Orders of Architecture by 66 carefully prepared plates," and finally "by Samuel Sloan, Author of the 'Model Architect' just published by J. P. Lippincott & Co., Philadelphia."

Nutt's letters, usually written at Winter Quarters, were most often lengthy covering a wide range of subjects. One series dealt with location of a dumbwaiter to carry food to the dining table. The original plans specified that it should rise directly to the dining room, while Dr. Nutt insisted it be relocated to reach the second-story pantry. Other such minute details were painstakingly discussed—the location of a cistern, the types of blinds to be installed in corner rooms, the placement of partitions, window frames and bay window brackets, and the exact location of the main stairway.

In one letter, dated March 12, 1860, Dr. Nutt noted that he had sent fifteen men and eight boys to the Longwood site to begin making bricks. Later communication transmitted his complaint that the local brick masons were proving slow and inefficient. Nutt then asked Sloan to send down from Philadelphia some mason craftsmen who could "stir up mine." [14] This appears to be the first instance where shoddy performance by local workers or the unavailability of the kinds of skills needed necessitated dispatching Philadelphia artisans to Natchez to carry on the building program.

Longwood: A New Idea

In May, 1861, the correspondence began to reflect the disruption in communications occasioned by the war. In a letter written in June, Sloan remarked that he had not heard from Dr. Nutt in four weeks, though letters between the two customarily reached their destinations in a week or less. Correspondence soon after halted altogether.

The Sloan–Nutt letters have been preserved in the Huntington Library in San Marino, California. The collection also includes a few documents written by other persons, such as the

The interior of the main floor of the house is virtually as it was left in 1861 when the Civil War started.

THE HERITAGE OF LONGWOOD

texts of agreements between craftsmen and either Sloan or Dr. Nutt. Among these is a note, published in a Natchez newspaper, which was written March 19, 1861, by four of the Pennsylvania craftsmen on their departure for home in the North. "Having terminated to *(sic)* brick work of Mr. Haller Nutt's mansion, we would take this method of tendering to that gentleman our sincere thanks for the very liberal and uniformly kind treatment extended to us during our sojourn with him; and to the citizens of Natchez generally, who have manifested to us the greatest courtesy during the intense excitement through which we have just passed." [15]

NOTES TO CHAPTER 1

1. Ina May Ogletree McAdams, *The Building of Longwood* (Austin: Private Publication, 1962), 1.
2. *Ibid.*, 2 ff.
3. Walter Lord, (ed.), *The Freemantle Diary: The South at War.* (Boston: Little, Brown and Company in cooperation with Bantam Books, 1954), 79, 80.
4. Harnett T. Kane, *Natchez on the Mississippi* (New York: Bonanza Books, 1967), 290.
5. O. S. Fowler, *A Home for All, Or the Gravel Wall and Octagon Mode of Building* (New York: Fowler and Wells, Publishers, 1853), frontispiece.
6. *Ibid.*, 82 f. Also referred to in Wayne Andrews, *Architecture, Ambition and Americans* (New York: Harper and Brothers, rev. ed., 1955), 124.
7. Marie T. Logan, *Mississippi-Louisiana Border Country: A History of Rodney, Mississippi, St. Joseph, Louisiana, and Environs.* (Baton Rouge: Claitor's Publishing Division, 1970), 234.
8. George L. Hersey, "Godey's Choice," *Journal of the Society of Architectural Historians,* 18 (October, 1959), 104.
9. *Ibid.*, 105.
10. Harold N. Cooledge, Jr. "A Sloan Checklist," *Journal of the Society of Architectural Historians,* 19; (March, 1960), 34–38.
11. McAdams, *The Building of Longwood,* 6, 11, 14, 18.
12. *Ibid.*, 14.
13. Samuel Sloan, *Sloan's Homestead Architecture* (Philadelphia: Lippincott, 186), 29.
14. McAdams, *The Building of Longwood,* 27.
15. *Ibid.*, 64. The note was signed by Charles Porter, Peter Willets, William L. Room, and Oliver Scharz.

Chapter 2

The People of Longwood

It has often been said that the story of architecture in the Old South just before the Civil War was largely, if not wholly, the chronicle of the newly rich. The Nutt family was the exception. They had not acquired new-found wealth to be superimposed on a background of little breeding. "Not every planter was so cultivated as Haller Nutt," wrote Wayne Andrews in *Architecture, Ambitions, and Americans.*[1]

Dr. Nutt's earliest known forebear was Cnut, or Knut, a Scandinavian with more than forty lordships recorded behind his name in *The Domesday Book,* the official listing of property owners in England and the lands they owned, at the time of King Edward the Confessor. The family was first mentioned in English heraldry as being situated in County Kent. An ancestor named Thomas Knutt of London was clerk patron and parson of Berwick. It was his son William who emigrated to Virginia in 1660 to establish the American branch of the family.[2]

A fifth-generation direct descendant of William was Dr. Rushworth Nutt, who shortened his first name to Rush in honor of Dr. Benjamin Rush, noted physician under whom he had studied medicine in Philadelphia. Dr. Rush Nutt, whose young first wife died after six months of marriage, was eventually wed a second time in Jefferson County, Mississippi, to Eliza Ker. Miss Ker was the daughter of Judge David Ker, of the state supreme court and founder and first presiding professor of Chapel Hill College in North Carolina. To Eliza and Rush were born several children, including sons Rittenhouse and Haller. Dr. Rush Nutt expected Rittenhouse to exhibit his own bent for scholarship and science, but it was Haller who did so.[3]

Portrait of Haller Nutt located at Longwood.

Portrait of Julia Nutt located at Longwood.

THE HERITAGE OF LONGWOOD

Haller was educated in Louisiana, Mississippi, Virginia, and at the University of Louisville, where he earned a degree in medicine. He then returned home to join his father in agriculture and to assist in scientific experiments. He helped make improvements in farm machinery and planting methods. The crude Whitney cotton gin was perfected by the two men, who also were among the first to advocate circular or horizontal plowing to prevent soil erosion. Like his father, Haller Nutt devoted a great deal of time and study to crossbreeding cotton strains, with the result that his superior crops brought exceedingly high prices on the market.[4]

Already the master of several plantations, Dr. Nutt in 1840 met pretty and vivacious Julia Augusta Williams, six years his junior. They were married at Evergreen Plantation in Louisiana that same year. He was 24 and she 18. Julia was an intellectually competent woman, proud and courageous, with as good an education as was available to women of that time. She and Dr. Nutt were deeply compatible in their relationship, which lasted for almost twenty-four years, until his death from pneumonia in 1864, at the age of 48. Eleven children were born to them and eight lived to adulthood. The youngest two were born at Longwood.[5]

In 1850, Dr. Nutt purchased Winter Quarters, a plantation on the shore of Lake St. Joseph in Louisiana that formerly had belonged to Julia's grandfather. Winter Quarters, as the name indicates, was the Nutts' home in the colder months.[6] During the planting and harvesting seasons, the Nutts spent much of their time in Louisiana, first on Araby plantation and later at Winter Quarters. Only in the Civil War Period after the devastation of Louisiana plantations did residence in Natchez begin.

For several years after his marriage, Dr. Nutt had spread the word that he was interested in purchasing the Natchez acreage on which was located an old house, also known as Longwood. Julia had often expressed fondness for the place because she had known so many happy hours there, visiting as a child with close friends. On September 18, 1850, Dr. Nutt was able to

The People of Longwood

complete the purchase of the 90-acre tract and 78.48 acres of land inside the city limits.[7] He also purchased 16.36 additional acres in Adams County. Not informing Julia of the sale just then, he made plans to surprise her.[8]

For some time the Nutt family had planned a trip to Natchez from Winter Quarters. Julia and the children were to visit with her parents at their Ashburn estate in Natchez, and Dr. Nutt was to attend to business affairs. The day arrived and the family was driven to Hard Times Landing on the Mississippi River to board a steamer that had a reputation as a follower of a leisurely timetable. In the end, a faster packet, which left somewhat earlier, was selected for part of the entourage. Dr. Nutt oversaw the loading of the house servants, some baggage, and many of his wife's personal belongings. When the slower steamer arrived at Natchez and the entire family was finally settled at Ashburn, Dr. Nutt suggested a drive to Longwood. Ostensibly, the ride would give Mrs. Nutt still another look at the place she had loved and which, she thought, was unoccupied. Julia was delighted and amazed to find her servants and possessions already in the old house waiting for her.[9]

By the time the Nutts decided to resettle in Natchez, it was a booming river city, bustling with commerce, shipping, and the wealth-building activities of cotton planters. But until 1716, when the French arrived, the town and area had been ruled by the Natchez Indian tribe. The settlement established by the French was destroyed in an uprising of the tribe in 1729, yet the town's growth continued. In 1776, the community consisted of ten log cabins, two frame houses, and four small stores, all in the area later to be known as Under-the-Hill, near the banks of the Mississippi.[10]

In 1776, Natchez marked the southern boundary of the United States. It was the most isolated of American settlements, forced by its location to be economically self-sufficient. As a frontier town, it had been ruled not only by the Indians and the French who succeeded them, but later by Spain and England. As an English possession, Natchez was in fact a fourteenth colony of Great Britain. The people of the town, however, remained neutral during the Revolutionary War, standing aside from the strife taking place along the Atlantic coast a thousand miles away. Because of its isolated location, Natchez was vulnerable to the aggressions of the Spanish governor of New Orleans, who took control of the town in 1779.[11]

Natchez experienced renewed growth and prosperity under a Spanish rule that history has judged to be efficient and fair. One of the Spaniards' legacies to Natchez was a love of pomp and lavish living; the first large homes rising on the bluffs overlooking the Mississippi reflected that love. The Spanish era lasted until 1798, when the last of the Spaniards left, and the Territory of Mississippi was formed, with Natchez as its capital, flying the American flag.

In the Mississippi volume of the W.P.A. state guide appears an excellent description of Natchez as the eighteenth century merged into the nineteenth: "A frontier city, capital of a rich territory, Natchez soon grew important as a supply depot and the gathering place for the intellectuals of the Southwest. It became an opulent, suave and aristocratic community, maintaining a social and political prestige that influenced the entire Mississippi Valley." [12]

Men of all degrees of ambition and intelligence were drawn to this new region where land was cheap and fortunes were made quickly. Hundreds of families, traveling in fleets of flatboats, drifted down the river from the upper valleys. The pioneers found a rich and fertile country that had a mild climate featured by a growing season nine months long. They tried raising indigo, but discovered it could not be grown because of refuse accumulation and poisonous drainage. Next, the newcomers tried growing tobacco; this venture too they found unprofitable. With the invention of Eli Whitney's cotton gin in 1793, they began growing cotton. Slave labor, along with natural advantages, enabled the entrepreneurs to create, in a remarkably short time in the nineteenth century, a system of great plantations and luxurious living. To give some idea of the

The People of Longwood

opulence of that period in southern history, it may be well to explain the extent of the menage of Dr. Nutt. He owned 800 farm slaves, 32 house servants, and a number of grooms and stablemen to care for Kentucky-bred horses. There were governesses for the Nutt girls and a tutor for the boys, with separate school buildings maintained for each.[13]

In December, 1859, the Nutt family consisted of Haller, Julia and seven children — Carrie Routh, 18; Mary Ella, 16; Haller, Jr., 13; Austin, 7; Sargeant Prentiss, 5; Julia Augusta, 2; and Calvin R., 1. In 1860 John Ker was born and in 1861 Lily. The Nutts had lost their little daughter Fanny Smith in 1848 while living at Araby plantation. In another family tragedy, Austin was accidentally shot to death by a cousin early in January, 1860.[14]

Dr. Nutt was a sober man who took his duties and obligations seriously. He felt deep concern for the approximately 800 slaves who worked his plantations[15] and cared for the family's homes. He never set up a medical practice, preferring agriculture and scientific invention, but records reveal that he would personally administer to his slaves when they were ill. He was known as a kind master, fair and just toward his blacks. One long-term man-servant named Uncle Frederick, who continued to care for Julia and the children after Dr. Nutt died, is buried in the family graveyard at Longwood alongside members of the family. (A newly restored portrait of the servant hangs in Longwood today.) So well did this master care for his slaves that:

> ... following the freeing of the slaves by Federal troops who first reached the area, and later by the Emancipation Proclamation, many who left Dr. Nutt later returned, asking to resume their places at the gins, in the sawmills or in planting and harvesting the crops; and they stayed on, serving Haller Nutt, until Federal armies had wrought their final havoc and everything of value including cattle and crops, outbuildings and quarters, gins, sawmills and boats had been confiscated or been put to the torch and gone up in smoke.[16]

The destruction of Haller's property was curiously anomalous. At least philosophically, Dr. Nutt was an acknowledged and strong Union sympathizer, if not an activist, on the side of the North.

In a biography of her husband, Union General Walter Quintin Gresham, Matilda Gresham reported on life in Natchez after August 26, 1863, when her husband was assigned to command the Third Brigade, Fourth Division, Seventeenth Army Corps, with headquarters at Rosalie on the bluff above the river. She noted that "from the first he was brought into close contact with the city's people."[17] General and Mrs. Gresham were accepted in the local society due to their "Southern background."[18] Haller Nutt was friendly with the northern occupiers of Natchez, and the Greshams were often entertained at Longwood. "Many times we dined there," wrote Mrs. Gresham.[19] The Nutts were considered Union people even though Dr. Nutt was from Virginia and owned hundreds of slaves. Mrs. Gresham described the Nutts' house:

> "Longwood," the Nutt home, was about a mile and a half out of Natchez to the southeast on the Woodville Road. When the war began, it was in the process of being built anew. The blockade stopped its construction as the roof and first story were completed. This first story and the house for the servants, a good dwelling for anyone, formed the Nutt abode in 1863 .... "Longwood's" eighty acres, with sixty servants, were well cared for. In the garden were five hundred varieties of roses. Miss Carrie Nutt was a charming young woman and deservedly popular with all, especially our young officers.[20]

NOTES TO CHAPTER 2

1. Andrews, *Architecture, Ambition and Americans*, 146.
2. Margaret Shields Hendrix, *The Legend of Longwood* (Natchez: Hudson Printing Company, 1972), 16.
3. *Ibid.*, 16-20.
4. *Bibliographical and Historical Memoirs of Mississippi*, (Chicago: The Goodspeed Publishing Company, 1891), II, 520.
5. McAdams, *The Building of Longwood*, 8.
6. Tradition holds that Winter Quarters was so named because its first owner, Job Routh, used it as a hunting and fishing camp. Logan, *Mississippi-Louisiana Border Country*, 230.
7. This transaction is recorded in Book HH, page 316, Adams County Court House, Natchez, Mississippi.

NOTES TO CHAPTER 2

8. Hendrix, *The Legend of Longwood*, 2.
9. Kane, *Natchez on the Mississippi*, 289; Hendrix, *The Legend of Longwood*, 2.
10. Kane, *Natchez on the Mississippi*, 3–21.
11. U.S. Federal Writers Project, *Mississippi: A Guide to the Magnolia State* (New York: Hastings House, 1949), 238.
12. *Ibid.*, 239.
13. Catherine Van Court, *In Old Natchez* (New York: Doubleday, Doran & Company, 1938), 106.
14. McAdams, *The Building of Longwood*, 8.
15. Haller Nutt owned a number of plantations. Laurel Hill in Jefferson County, Mississippi, where he had been born, was inherited from his father. There were three properties in Louisiana — Araby, Winter Quarters, and Evergreen. Besides Longwood, there was also Cloverdale plantation about four miles from Natchez.
16. Hendrix, *The Legend of Longwood*, 19.
17. Matilda Gresham, *Life of Walter Quintin Gresham* (Chicago: Rand McNally & Company, 1919), I, 241.
18. Theodora Brinton Marshall and Gladys Crail Evans, *They Found It in Natchez* (Natchez: The Reliquary, 1946), 163.
19. Gresham, *The Life of Walter Quintin Gresham*, 247.
20 *Ibid.*

Chapter 3

The Octagon Concept

One of the more novel features of Longwood was its octagonal form. O. S. Fowler, in his *Home for All or the Gravel Wall and Octagon Mode of Building,* published in 1853, and Samuel Sloan, in *Sloan's Homestead Architecture* (1861), detailed widely divergent points of view about the possible uses of octagon-shaped housing. Fowler sought to bring homes within the economic reach of all. "To cheapen and improve human homes, and especially to bring comfortable dwellings within the reach of the poorer classes, is the object of this volume — an object of the highest practical utility to man," he wrote. "It delineates a new mode of enclosing public edifices and private residences, far better, every way, and several hundred percent cheaper, than any other." He added that the octagonal home "will enable the poor but ingenious man to erect a comfortable dwelling at a trifling cost." [1]

Sloan, by contrast, began his text for a chapter on "Design I, An Oriental Villa," by writing: "We enter upon our series [on homestead architecture] by the presentation of a design adapted to the wants of the man of fortune in any section." The design, he noted, was "particularly suitable for the home of a retired Southern planter." [2] He continued:

> Aside from the novelty of the plan, it has every recommendation for convenience and utility that can be devised for a residence, where not only comfort but luxury is destined to reign. The occupants of such a residence are not only supposed to be wealthy, but fashionable people, and to possess in common with all the real aristocracy of every section, a character for hospitality, exhibited in the frequent entertainment of numerous guests, and a liberal allowance of time and money for the purpose of social and convivial enjoyment.[3]

Air view of the house and grounds. Note the unusual roof plan. To the right of the house is the servants' quarters. Haller and Julia Nutt lived there while Longwood was under construction.

The Octagon Concept

Both men, one an amateur architect and the other a full-fledged professional, appear to have had the same advantage of the octagon design in mind — more interior space. Fowler's poor man would have more area in which his large family could live without cramping. Sloan's wealthy aristocrat would have the same kind of space, but for another, entirely different life.

In his section on what he called the superiority of the octagon form, Fowler posed a double question — is the square form the best of all? is the right angle the best angle? "Cannot some radical improvement be made, both in the outside form and the internal arrangement of our houses?" he asked. "Nature's forms are mostly spherical. Then why not apply her forms to houses? Since a circle encloses more space for its surface than any other form, of course, the nearer spherical our houses, the more inside room for the outside wall, besides being more comfortable." [4]

Sloan's plans for Longwood had called for a separate kitchen building to cater food to the Nutts and their guests. Fowler would have nothing to do with such a concept. Revealing his sense of empathy with the proletariat, he wrote:

> The kitchen of the octagon deserves especial remark. The kitchen is the stomach of the house. Shall it then be thrust away back out of doors, into another building? This would be like putting the human stomach away down in the feet. In the octagon kitchen the wife, when she leaves the sitting-room to attend to kitchen duties — pleasures — instead of feeling that she is going away off alone out of doors, feels that she is only a step removed from the rest of the family. What say you, wives, to this? [5]

As if this were not enough, Fowler proclaimed the fundamental sightliness of the American kitchen. "The sight of a tidy kitchen is not so very disgusting, even to men of refined tastes," he commented. "None who are not too extra nice, fastidious and fashionable to eat, but like the sight of the kitchen" — except, perhaps, for those "double-exquisite" ladies who are "as cordially disgusted with household duties as with good sense." [6]

Carpenters and restorers admire the wonderful craftsmanship of Sloan's millwork for Longwood.

Wooden ornament for the house was made in Philadelphia and shipped to Natchez. See Figure 8.

Drop pendants beneath the roof eave.

Even the chimneys of Longwood incorporate Moorish arches in their design.

THE HERITAGE OF LONGWOOD

Samuel Sloan, often a vehement spokesman for the importance of the architect in building, was also an able exponent of adaptation of the ancient design to contemporary styles. In his chapter, "Remarks on Style," he wrote: "When we speak of a building being in the Grecian, Italian, Gothic or any of the numerous well-known sub-styles, we mean that the spirit rather than the sum total of the peculiarities of that style has been seized upon and infused into it. No design... can be pointed out as a facsimile of any ancient or foreign specimen of architecture; but ancient forms and details have too long appealed to the tastes or prejudices of mankind for the architect to dream of their abandonment." [7]

"The orator or poet would not be more subject to blame for laying aside the teachings of the past than would the architect for neglecting the precedents set before him in the works of ancient masters," Sloan explained. "Instead of eloquence and poetry, the... audience would be fed on the rudiments of an unintelligible language; and instead of a pleasing combination of forms resulting in the most happy effects, unmeaning piles of brick and stone at every step would greet our vision." [8]

Sloan may have had his Oriental villa in mind when he continued, "The popular mind is easily reached through a medium combining beauty of aspect with antiquity of origin; it is affected by an appreciation of the present interwoven with a veneration for the past." [9]

When the dwelling of the private citizen finally became a subject for the display of taste and genius of the architect, Sloan felt the architect naturally enough looked to the most magnificent specimens of ancient or contemporary public architecture for guidance in the selection of forms and details. "As a consequence we see domestic buildings, even down to modern times (the mid-19th century) wearing the exact dress of the heathen temple, or the livery of the medieval church or castle. By degrees, however, domestic architecture is improving, and that improvement is accelerated by copying nothing ancient or foreign further than its application... in strict consonance with the requirements of domestic life." [10]

Compare the window decorations as completed in 1861 with Sloan's original designs of 1852 as seen in Figure 5.

The galleries, alternating with the Moorish windows, have a Venetian quality in their lightness.

The Octagon Concept

In other words, apparently, the octagonal oriental villa adapted exterior style features from earlier times, but inside was a residence to be lived in, one accommodated to the life style and comfort of its inhabitants. Sloan cited an incident in line with his thinking:

> In passing by a fine residence... a friend inquired whether it was a church, college or court house, which we were not able to answer until we approached close enough to determine by the drapery in the windows that it was a dwelling house.
>
> It was a classic building and a fine specimen of architecture, but was it domestic architecture? Some one has very well said that the ancient practice should be treated as a servant, not as a master. Without doubt the gentlemanly proprietor of the classic house would have scorned to receive from the painter's hand the picture of Apollo as his own portrait, and yet he has permitted his architect to disguise, under the semblance of a heathen temple, the real character of his place of residence.[11]

The plans for Longwood were published in *Godey's Lady's Book and Magazine* in January, 1861 (Figure 7), after the Nutt home was under construction. Calling it a villa in the oriental style, Sloan noted above the picture that the building had been "designed expressly" for the magazine. He commented on the novelty of the idea and how it was being adopted to a southern climate as well as mentioning that it was "in process of erection at Natchez, Mississippi." The illustration shows the exterior as it might have been with trees and gardens around. The architectural detail is remarkably similar to that which was built; much of it can still be seen today.

Below the picture Sloan reproduced plans for the basement and principal story. On the next page, the plan for the second story appeared. The plan was "essentially an x with trapezoidal spaces between the arms filled in with verandas, so that the exterior assumes the shape of an octagon."[12] The room arrangement had one shape and the porches gave another to the building. "The central quality of the plan is followed relentlessly in the matter of door placement." The complexity seen at Longwood gained further development after the Civil War as verandas increased in popularity, but, these developments had

FIGURE 7. The design for Longwood published in *Godey's Lady's Book*, Vol. LXII, 1861. This picture gives the best idea of what the house would have looked like when finished. Although only a simple woodcut, the picture has been of great help to 20th Century restorers.

The Octagon Concept

"an inner coherence which reveals order in a place where many have thought that chaos reigned supreme."[13]

The choice of an architectural style for the oriental villa, Sloan explained, did not come about by accident but by design. That choice was "less a matter of caprice than the natural outgrowth of the ground plan adopted." He added, "The central apartment, designed as it was, not only for a thoroughfare by which all adjacent rooms could be entered, besides being so favorably situated as a medium for light and ventilation, naturally suggested the domed observatory. Fancy dictated that the dome should be bulbiform — a remembrancer *(sic.)* of Eastern magnificence which few will judge misplaced as it looms up against the mellow azure of a Southern sky."[14]

After describing the floor plans of the multistoried villa, Sloan also wrote that it would be difficult to conceive a plan in which the abstract elements of strength were more successfully combined than in the one "now under construction" [Longwood].[15] By their peculiar relative positions, he felt, the walls would mutually strengthen and sustain each other to such a degree as to defy the storms of a torrid climate.

In offering the oriental villa design, Sloan nonetheless avoided any definite estimate of its possible cost. Such an estimate could not be made, he declared, "without entering into a more specific description of the execution of both the interior and exterior." Location had much to do with it: "In this part of the Middle [Atlantic] States, however, assuming the walls to be built of good brick, the exterior stuccoed and the interior finished in a manner consistent with the general character of the design and hints we have given, ... the total cost would not vary much from $40,000."[16]

NOTES TO CHAPTER 3

1. Fowler, *A Home for All*, iii.
2. Sloan, *Sloan's Homestead Architecture*, 57.
3. *Ibid.*
4. Fowler, *A Home for All*, 82.
5. *Ibid.*, 99.

NOTES TO CHAPTER 3

6. Fowler, *A Home for All*, 99.
7. Sloan, *Sloan's Homestead Architecture*, 25.
8. *Ibid.*
9. *Ibid.*, 26.
10. *Ibid.*, 28.
11. *Ibid.*, 28–29.
12. Hersey, "Godey's Choice," 108.
13. *Ibid.*, 111.
14. Sloan, *Sloan's Homestead Architecture*, 57-58.
15. *Ibid.*, 60.
16. *Ibid.*, 62.

Chapter 4

The Construction of Longwood

Dr. Nutt notified Sloan by letter on December 24, 1859, that the family was ready to start building. On January 11, 1860, the architect replied that he had made all arrangements to leave for the South "next Tuesday," and hoped to reach Natchez about a week later.[1] Sloan did make the trip; subsequent letters from Dr. Nutt so indicate—communications in which the physician expressed his regret that, due to illness, he had been unable to meet with him. The architect made at least one more trip to the site in April, 1860.

The first building on the grounds of the "new" Longwood was the spacious three-story servants' quarters, a structure intended eventually to provide accommodations for the 32 slaves who would care for the mansion. The Nutt family lived in this smaller building when the old home was demolished and construction of the new one had begun.

Although Dr. Nutt and his wife had altered some of the original specifications for Longwood as prepared and presented by architect Sloan, the building was constructed essentially as planned. The specifications (see Appendix) went into exhaustive detail, not only as regards floor plan and building dimensions, but also concerning the sizes and types of materials to be used. High ceilings were specified—9 feet in height for the basement, 14 feet for the principal story, 12 for the second floor, and 9 for the third. In addition, the central rotunda would rise the full height of the building. The depth of the excavation was determined by the specified height of the basement floor.

THE HERITAGE OF LONGWOOD

A note from the specifications shows how precisely developed were the details of construction: "The joists for the first and second floors and corresponding verandas and galleries will be 8 by 10 inches, those for the third floor 8 by 10 inches, for the upper galleries 3 by 9 inches, the ceiling joists throughout 3 by 8 and the studding required for the wood partitions 3 by 4 inches and all placed 16 inches between centres." [2]

Plans also called for the cupola to be framed with 5 by 7 inch posts of scantling extending from the fourth floor. The

The first floor interior in 1936 showing boarded up windows, niches for sculptures, and boxed window frames which admitted light to the basement.

The view up to the dome today shows only rough framing and temporary walkways.

framing of the dome atop the cupola "will be in accordance with the drawings and secured where necessary with one-inch iron bolts and the necessary straps."[3]

All floors, the specifications indicated, would be of "5/4 inch heart pine," mill-worked and well seasoned boards securely nailed to the joists and sanded off later. Floors for the hall adjoining the veranda and the rotunda were to be inlaid with "marble filings."[4]

Several staircases were never built because construction was halted by the war. One such was a flight of geometrical stairs in the front hall. Its handrail and newel were to have been of black walnut, its balusters of light-colored wood. A flight of stairs was also planned on the rear veranda from the basement to the second floor, and another, within the building, from the second to the third floor. A small flight of stairs was to lead from the third floor to the gallery above.

All the windows were to have one and three-quarter inch thick sashes, "double hung with the best-patent cord, weights and sham—axle pullies."[5] Windows opening on the verandas on the first floor were to extend entirely to the floor, all opening to the balconies. All second floor windows would terminate six inches above the floor.

Doors for the principal story were to be exclusively walnut and all the others throughout of white pine. Doors opening on the veranda were two and one-half inches thick—folding doors hung with four-by-four inch butts. Sliding doors opening on the rotunda were to be of the same thickness, and would move on six-inch sheaves with brass ways.

The specifications paid special attention to the roofing: "The roof will be overlaid with one cross-leaded roofing tin, painted on both sides, the upper side to have two coats. The dome will be covered with sheet lead properly secured and ribbed. All the gutters to be formed so as to convey the water to eight-inch conductors placed at the intersection of the verandas with the wings—these will be iron and connect with a pipe leading to the cistern placed over the kitchen."[6]

Guesswork about plastering was also ruled out. All the walls

The Construction of Longwood

and ceilings throughout, including the dome, were to be plastered with two coats of brown mortar and one of white, hard finish. The mortar for plastering was "to be composed of clean sharp sand and fresh lime properly proportioned and well mixed with 'slaughtered hair'."[7]

Either Sloan or Nutt, or both, regarded marble and silver as marks of quality. For example, the bathtub was to have a paneled front, "neatly filled up" and "lined with copper-tinned and planished." But the wash basin was to have a counter-sunk marble top with a door beneath. "All fixtures will be silver plated," and marble mantles "of neat and approved pattern" were to be set to each fireplace.[8] More silver-plating was planned elsewhere, including hinges and knobs on the first floor and the bellpull at the front door. Knobs in other parts of the house were to be white porcelain.

Longwood's dimensions permitted especially spacious and high-ceilinged rooms—planned to total thirty-two in all. Had the first, or principal, floor been completed, it would have had an octagonal rotunda 24 feet in diameter and a main entrance hall, with principal staircase, measuring 20 by 34 feet. The front veranda was designed with dimensions of 12 by 40 feet.

Other room sizes in the original drawings were as follows, given in feet:

> Drawing room, 20 by 34
> Reception room, 18 by 24
> Family room, 18 by 24
> Second family room, 20 by 34
> Third family room, 18 by 24
> Breakfast room, 20 by 34 [9]

Construction of the new Longwood went ahead steadily. In early 1860, slaves had begun erecting the 27-inch-thick walls that would insulate against both summer heat and winter chill. Sometime later, artisans were hired from the North to do carpentry and other jobs requiring journeyman skills.

Estimates vary on the actual total cost of Longwood, but one that appears reliable places it at almost $28,000, excluding the

Lath and framing in the upper stories shows the complexity of Longwood's construction. Modern carpenters envy the skill demonstrated here.

The exposed framework of the gigantic dome looms six stories above the visitor's head.

costs of land and home furnishings. This estimate was derived from analysis of the architect's bill of particulars, and was based on the prices of labor and materials prevailing at the time. For example, excavation for the immense building cost only $250. The bricks used in construction were baked of native clay on the site and cost only $10 per thousand. Plastering was a mere 20 cents a yard. Doors cost, on the average, only $4 each. [10]

The overall height of Longwood was more than 100 feet. Each of the eight sides extended for 37 lineal feet, for a total circumference of 296 feet. The building's diameter was about 100 feet. Other facts and statistics indicate the grand scale on which planning was carried out:

—The first floor was to include dressing rooms and side and rear verandas.

—The basement floor was not designed to serve as living quarters; instead, plans called for the rotunda angle spaces to be occupied by closets, with the remainder of the available basement space to accommodate an office, smoking room, school rooms, a storeroom, a playroom, and a servants' hall.

—There were to be six bedrooms (called chambers), most of them measuring 17 by 20 feet, on the second floor along with a bath, two dressing rooms, a pair of wardrobes, and four verandas.

—Three more chambers, each with a fireplace, were to be found on the third floor. For some reason, these bedrooms were larger than the rest, almost 21 by 34 feet. A trunk room of the same size was also projected.

—Among the innovations of the new Longwood was a fireplace venting system that had never been employed before. Because the fireplaces were in what otherwise would be wasted space, four circular chimney shafts, two-and-a-half feet in diameter, were to be built; each one would be built to the full height of the residence. Sloan described this venting method as both economical and thoroughly efficient.

—Pipes for water and gas were concealed within the walls. The mansion was to be lighted by gas, and water from the roof was to be conveyed from the roof to an iron cistern situated over a two-story brick kitchen.

The Construction of Longwood

—In all, some 754,000 bricks went into Longwood's exterior. All of them were believed to have been made on the property in kilns which were among the first projects ordered completed by Dr. Nutt when construction was imminent. Four expert Philadelphia bricklayers were brought down to Natchez to work with the slaves.

—White and yellow pine for the joists, rafters, and scaffolding was cut locally at the Andrew Brown sawmill in Natchez. Piles of cypress went into the exterior woodwork.

Brown's sawmill was commissioned by Dr. Nutt to cut most of the lumber for Longwood. One formidable order to the Natchez mill was for 50,000 feet of one-inch plank twelve to eighteen inches wide and sixteen to twenty feet long. Yet another order, this one dated November 29, 1860, asked Andrew Brown "for a few more pieces of timber for the Cupulo (sic) of the house." Haller needed fourteen pieces 38 feet long and 5 by 7 inches, "as early as you can—made of good cypress." [11]

By the end of the Civil War, and certainly during the time Nutt needed its services for Longwood, Andrew Brown's sawmill was very successful in the Lower Mississippi Valley. Production of cypress lumber must have been one of its most profitable operations. The wood's durability was, of course, its main attraction for consumers, but from a sawmill owner's point of view, it had an added advantage: sawyers using two-man handsaws could manufacture cypress boards easily because the wood was comparatively free of resin and was almost as soft to handle as white pine. For the same reasons, carpenters found that cypress boards did not warp when used green. Of equal importance, cypress, probably due to its low resin content, was much less flammable than yellow pine, its chief competitor. [12]

Most of the cypress at Longwood is still intact today, hardly damaged by more than a century of Mississippi weather. The wooden 25-foot flagpole atop the dome, however, did fall, but it was made of pine. The pole was probably the victim of woodpeckers, which, incidentally, cannot penetrate cypress.

Tin for the roof was ordered in Philadelphia from Cumming

and Brodie, Metal Composition and Gravel Roofers, on May 26, 1860. Boxes of tin "making 121 Bundles," seventy-five pounds of solder, and one barrel of clamps came to a total of $853.25. A "tinner," Jacob Walters, was among the skilled workmen imported to install the roof.[13]

Other materials for Longwood can be ascertained from numerous bills of lading. Samuel Sloan ordered the building materials and had them sent to New Orleans where they were placed on the levee to await transfer to a river boat for Natchez. On the second of May, 1860, he sent seventy wooden window frames and seven boxes of marble window sills which were received in New Orleans July 12 to be forwarded to Natchez. Stone work for the mansion—including four marble door sills, twelve window sills, and four Picton stone caps for the chimneys—was carved by Edwin Greble in Philadelphia. Seventy-three window frames, seven sills, fifty-four kegs of nails and a "lot of slates said to weigh three tons," [these intended for the foundation floor and basement], were shipped May 26, also reaching New Orleans July 12. Lime was sent on the 28th of July marked on the bill of lading as "thirty four Hds Lime on Deck," but when it was received in New Orleans or Natchez is not known.[14]

Sloan referred to the lime shipment in a letter written July 30, 1860. Explaining difficulties he had encountered in shipping the building materials, particularly the "rough and careless handling," Sloan added that he could not "understand why you receive no bill of lading from New Orleans to Natchez in the regular course of things." The letter, which is filled with apologies to Nutt for shipping problems, ended with the notation that "the lime is shipped to the same," and that the bills of lading would be sent soon.

It has often been assumed that the wooden architectural ornament for Longwood's exterior was made on the site by local workmen following directions sent by Samuel Sloan. "Patterns," many of which are in the house today, were, in fact, made in Philadelphia. A "Bill of Materials," (Figure 8) as well as bills of lading for New Orleans and Natchez, prove that

Bill of Materials

Delivered on board Ship Villa Franco for Haller Nutt, Natchez.

August 27th 1860.

Qty	Item	Unit Price	Total
99	Columns	at $17.00	$1683.00
16	Windowframes 13 ft long	23.00	368.00
16	" " 4 " "	4.00	64.00
1	" " 11 " "	48.00	48.00
2	" " 8.6 inches "	46.00	92.00
105	Turned bases	1.50	157.50
7	Fluted pilasters	6.00	42.00
106	Trusses over columns	6.00	636.00
56	First story brackets	5.00	280.00
76	Pieces of drapery	3.50	266.00
56	Second story brackets	4.00	224.00
76	Pieces of drapery 2d story	2.00	152.00
16	Brackets for basement	6.50	104.00
1900	feet bracket moulding	.04	76.00
1900	" fillet for brackets	.03	57.00
1300	" Washboard moulding	.06	78.00
1300	" Moulding under rail	.04	52.00
1300	" Fillet	.03	39.00
650	" Plank rail	.05	32.50
325	" Bevel caps	.04	13.00
325	" Moulded	.06	19.50
143	Pedestals	7.50	1072.50
	Total		$5556.00

FIGURE 8. The bill of materials for the millwork for Longwood. This document shows that the wooden decoration was fabricated in Philadelphia and shipped to Natchez to be installed on the house.

Piles of cutout work still remain in the house today. Formerly thought to be "patterns," they are actually pieces of decoration never installed on the building.

Freshly painted by a national retail paint firm, Longwood's woodwork has been preserved in all its splendor.

THE HERITAGE OF LONGWOOD

all the architectural fancy work was shipped in. It came to New Orleans in 116 boxes on the ship *Villa France*, arriving on September 29, 1860, when it was consigned to Haller Nutt. The bill for shipment to Natchez is dated the 11th of October. Most of the ornament can still be seen in place or piled in corners of the upper stories of the mansion.

On May 19, 1861, Haller Nutt wrote Sloan in Philadelphia describing the house as almost finished on the outside. "The finish is all painted, sanded and up; the Dome complete—brackets all up except in the lower cornice and most of the

FIGURE 9. Lithograph of Longwood published by J. F. Watson, S. E. Corner 4th and Walnut Sts., Philadelphia. Undated. Copies of this lithograph were handed out by Haller Nutt to friends curious about his house.

The Construction of Longwood

cornice complete to all the upper parts. It is creating much admiration now altho (sic) so much to interest us. I think after this the Octagon will be the style."[15] The lower cornice brackets are still missing today, although there are now plans to place them where they were designed to be on the finished mansion.

A picture of the house, as if completed, was published by J. F. Watson in Philadelphia (Figure 9). Clearly showing the architectural detail, it has been used by recent restorers to replace the cornice brackets, moldings, and other details. In the letter of May 19, 1861, Nutt asked Sloan to send twenty-five more of these lithographs. Nutt must have been passing them out to his friends to show how the house would appear when finished.

NOTES TO CHAPTER 4

1. McAdams, *The Building of Longwood*, 10.
2. *Ibid.*, 43.
3. *Ibid.*
4. *Ibid.*, 44.
5. *Ibid.*
6. *Ibid.*, 45.
7. *Ibid.*, 46.
8. *Ibid.*, 46-47.
9. *Ibid.*, 89.
10. *Ibid.*, 7.
11. *Ibid.*, 24.
12. John Hebron Moore, *Andrew Brown and Cypress Lumbering in the Old Southwest* (Baton Rouge: Louisiana State University Press, 1967), 5.
13. McAdams, *The Building of Longwood*, 74.
14. *Ibid.*, 60.
15. *Ibid.*, 67.

Chapter 5

The Furnishings of Longwood

By early 1861 the house was almost half finished. The outer structure, with its ornate colonnades and balconies, had already cost Dr. Nutt considerable sums, but he appropriated an approximately equal amount for marble stairs and statuary, rare tapestries, and other high quality appointments. The furnishings proposed for the house were to be as splendid as possible. Sloan's *Homestead Architecture* gives an idea of the decor as he visualized it in 1861 when the house was nearing completion. There were to be niches for statuary, "thus affording an excellent opportunity for tasteful decoration," and the upper alcoves, when duly decorated with plaster and drapery, "would be pleasant indeed."[1] The original conception for the interior can be seen in the *Model Architect* of 1851 (Figure 4).

Few of the orders sent, or contemplated, for luxurious materials have been found. A letter of July 30, 1861, from Sloan to Haller Nutt mentions that "the tile drawing has not yet been returned from England."[2] Tile floors were very fashionable at the time. Sloan felt tile was superior for vestibules and halls, its beauty suffering little "from abrasion of the colors in the long course of years." It was also easily cleaned. Had the tiles ever been installed in Longwood, their "gay and lively effect" would have been featured on the porch and front hall. The tiles were probably ordered from S. A. Harrison, 1010 Chestnut Street, Philadelphia, whose name and address appear above a colored drawing of various patterns of tiles in *Homestead Architecture*. In the same book, Sloan, writing about the projected oriental villa, recommends a special design for the central floor, "embracing a center flower...surrounded by regularly disposed patterns in bright, but not glaring colors." He noted that glass floor lights could be "inwrought" among the tiles without harming the design.[3]

As well as being an architect, Sloan was a "tastemaker" of the first order. His writings are full of advice for the homeowner on how to obtain tasteful suroundings, and many of his books even include advertisements for various firms. *Homestead Architecture* has a concluding chapter on furniture in which Sloan counsels "Lavish expenditure on ornament does not always produce the effect desired, and many rooms, where luxury without taste predominates, only serve to display the wealth of the owner." The architect often guided his customers in the selection of their furnishings, as he mentioned in a letter to Nutt written July 30, 1860. After a discussion of breakage of items in shipments, Sloan added, "Finding Col. Ventreys in the city (Philadelphia) . . . with his Ladie (sic) and with whom I felt warm obligation to render some attention as they wished to make purchase of furniture, etc., for their new house. This occupied all my time Saturday and also on Monday."[4]

The main supplier of Sloan's furnishings was the firm of George Henkels, the renowned Philadelphia cabinetmaker. From 1857 to 1862, Henkels' firm was located at 524 Walnut Street in the fashionable shopping section of Philadelphia. Henkels too was a "tastemaker" who had published *An Essay on Household Furniture,* an illustrated booklet of sixteen pages. His writing curiously paralleled the furniture writings of Samuel Sloan. Twelve engravings of furniture in *Homestead Architecture* are "particularly valuable documents of the taste of 1861."[5] From these pictures we may obtain the best idea of the furniture Haller Nutt chose for Longwood. From September 28 to October 1, 1860, during a visit to Philadelphia, Nutt probably made the final selection of the furniture. Several extant order cards offer a tantalizing peek at the proposed furnishings but are unfortunately not very specific. However, from the plates in *Homestead Architecture* (Figures 10, 11, 12, 13) and the simple notations on the cards, some conclusions may be drawn.

The Furnishing of Longwood

Sloan wrote that the illustrations in his book were drawn from original pieces in Henkels' stock. Showing prominent articles required in each room, the plates detail forms and shapes very well. The order card for the library [6] lists two bookcases, one table, four chairs, one lounge, and one step chair, all in the antique style (Figures 11, 12). According to Sloan, antique was not a style "exclusively its own, but is borrowed from most of the other distinctive styles."[7] He thought the antique style particularly appropriate to libraries. Haller Nutt's choices for his library were probably similar to those items pictured, as indeed his order card indicates.

The cards for the parlor furniture[8] list "Rosewood" pieces: a large sofa, two medium sofas, fourteen chairs, a center table, an étagére, two inlaid cabinets, and a grand piano. Cornices, curtains, mantle mirrors, carpet, and a rug were noted but unspecified as to style or price. The center table (Figure 10), which was priced at $1,700.00, may have been similar to the one illustrated, about which Sloan wrote that it ordinarily had a marble top, but that it could also have a clear plate glass lid in frame with the inside lined with velvet. He concluded that the resulting effect was quite good. Haller Nutt ordered the highest style pieces and spared no expense. The items he ordered for the Longwood dining room probably were similar to Sloan's picture (Figure 13). The description on this order card, however, gives only a general idea of the style. All the furniture listed would have cost $12,366, but this did not include carpet, drapes, and the like which would have been billed later.

The Nutts were prominent members of the Natchez community as well as Louisiana society. They already owned fine furnishings. The Henkels order was for things befitting their new house with its thirty splendid rooms. Julia and Haller Nutt had been married for ten years before they purchased the Longwood property in 1850. They had owned a number of properties and both had come from wealthy families. Julia's parents, the Williams, had a home furnished in grand style with mirrors, paintings, and chandeliers from abroad. Haller

FIGURE 10. Plate from Sloan's *Homestead Architecture* of 1861. The center table is doubtless similar to the one Haller Nutt ordered for Longwood.

FIGURE 11. "... and one step chair, all in the Antique Style."

FIGURE 12. Further examples of the Antique style from Sloan's *Homestead Architecture* indicate Haller Nutt's taste in furnishings.

FIGURE 13. Haller Nutt's choice of dining room furniture was probably similar to these pieces pictured in *Homestead Architecture*.

THE HERITAGE OF LONGWOOD

and Julia Nutt moved in the best circles and must have owned furniture in keeping with the times and their wealth.

In a letter of July 25, 1861 [9], Samuel Sloan wrote Nutt that he "took the responsibility of forewarding the foremost articles of furniture which you will require," adding, "I hope that our intercourse will soon be renewed but God only knows what is to be done as the War spirit predominates here." No trace remains of these pieces of furniture, for the blockade of Southern trade had by this time disrupted commerce. Matilda Gresham wrote that "the interior woodwork and furnishings then at sea, never reached Natchez." [10] This has been the accepted story and is still the only plausible explanation for the missing furniture.

The blockade of Southern ports had been announced on April 14, 1861, a few days after President Lincoln called for troops. Intended to destroy the trade of the South—particularly in and out of New Orleans, the principal commercial port and outlet of the Mississippi River—Lincoln's order was only partly successful. The unique position of New Orleans was appreciated by both sides, and Northern blockade efforts concentrated on that city. "For both North and South the fact that a well knit economic unit had been suddenly broken in two was fraught with the most perplexing consequences." [11] The United States government's policies were vague at best and trade regulations were difficult for anyone to untangle from a maze of acts of Congress and rules and regulations from the Treasury Department. Since definite measures were announced during the late spring and early summer of 1861, however, it seems very strange that Samuel Sloan should have attempted to send furniture to Natchez. On July 13, Congress declared that all commercial activity would cease, "when the president should by proclamation so order." [12] But the effect of this act was softened by allowing Lincoln to adjust the measure as he saw fit. The blockade of Southern ports, particularly New Orleans, was only partly effective, but it did disrupt trade and Sloan certainly should have realized this fact. The architect must have felt that these "foremost articles" would get through

The Furnishing of Longwood

the blockade, but such optimism was rare that summer. On August 16, Lincoln issued a definite proclamation, "declaring all commercial intercourse with insurrectionary regions at an end." Haller Nutt's furniture disappeared in the confusion.

The mirrors currently in the parlor and dining room of Longwood are, according to Natchez legend, part of Julia's wedding dowry, as is the four-poster bed given by her parents. The present piano, its crate still in existence, came from New Orleans. The face plate is now gone, but the lettering read: "Manufactured expressly for the Steiff Piano Company, Royal Street, New Orleans, La." Other packing crates on the upper floors and in corners of the servants' quarters are marked "Julia Nutt," but none has a Henkels label. Most of the existing

The crate for the Steiff piano is on the main floor while the instrument is still in the basement living quarters.

Trunks and suitcases are piled in odd corners of the unfinished house. Note the initials H. N., Haller Nutt.

furniture at Longwood can be documented to old Natchez families or has been donated by Pilgrimage Garden Club members.

Some misconceptions have arisen about the Longwood furnishings due to a description of the basement living quarters in Elizabeth Dunbar Murray's little book, *My Mother Used to Say*.[13] The Dunbar family left their plantation every summer and often rented a house in Natchez. In 1868 they "negotiated, with Mrs. Knutt (*sic*) for the use of Longwood." Describing the house, Mrs. Murray's mother said, "The family occupied the first floor which is handsomely furnished in mahogany and rosewood, and adorned with large mirrors and oil paintings." Most old families of Natchez retained in 1868 many fine pieces of furniture and the things currently at the house would fit this description.

The last actual record of furniture for Longwood comes in a paragraph in a letter from Samuel Sloan to Haller Nutt dated October 1, 1863: "Mr. Henkels sends his respects and hopes yet that he may have the pleasure of furnishing the new house.

The Furnishing of Longwood

He is now in Chestnut Street and occupies the store that Levy had when you were here. He makes a grand display. I suppose the finest in the whole country—or ANY COUNTRY. He is doing an immense business. Chestnut Street has wonderfully improved since your visit." [14]

The "foremost articles" have never been found and no record exists of their whereabouts. None of the furniture currently in the living quarters or basement of Longwood remotely resembles the magnificent pieces shown in Sloan's *Homestead Architecture*. Only one labeled Henkels piece has been found to date but careful examination does not reveal any at Longwood today.

NOTES TO CHAPTER 5

1. McAdams, *The Building of Longwood*, 89.
2. *Ibid.*, 71.
3. Sloan, *Sloan's Homestead Architecture*, 62, 262.
4. *Ibid.*, 54.
5. Kenneth Ames, "George Henkels, Nineteenth Century Philadelphia Cabinetmaker," *Antiques* (October, 1973), 641, 644.
6. McAdams, 77.
7. Sloan, *Homestead Architecture*, 324.
8. McAdams, *The Building of Longwood*, 76.
9. *Ibid.*
10. Gresham, *Life of Walter Quintin Gresham*, 247.
11. Coulter E. Merton, "Commercial Intercourse with the Confederacy in the Mississippi Valley, 1861–1865," *The Mississippi Valley Historical Review* (March 1901), 377.
12. *Ibid.*, 379.
13. Elizabeth Dunbar Murray, *My Mother Used to Say* (Boston: The Christopher Publishing House, 1959), 215–19.
14. McAdams, *The Building of Longwood*, 93.

Chapter 6

War and Aftermath

By the end of September, 1861, the mansion's exterior was almost complete, but little had been finished inside. Of the projected total of twenty-six fireplaces, only eight had been installed, and those were in the basement which, incidentally, Dr. Nutt had ordered raised almost to the height of a full story.

Although most of the mansions built in Natchez after 1700 employed armoires rather than clothes closets for wardrobe storage, Nutt did not consider these adequate for his family's needs. In all, he proposed twenty-four built-in closets; only four of these exist today, and all are on the basement level. For the west verandas of the principal and bedchamber floors, he also projected four large enclosed dressing rooms for the convenience of visitors and family members. And, in the rotunda of the first level, four spacious wine closets were planned instead of the conventional wine cellars found in most other homes of the time.

Plans for the completed building had called for some 115 doors, including those for closets, baths, and dressing and storage rooms.[1] The basement, finished for use as living quarters when the war forced changes in construction plans, today has thirty large doors. All were apparently installed in the midst of the pressures generated by the war, probably in the period between February and July, 1862, after the northern artisans had fled. In this period, Dr. Nutt enlisted his own slaves to finish the eight-room basement level. The interior walls were plastered and the slate originally ordered for the floors was replaced with cypress. Upstairs all the doors and many windows were boarded up and sealed.

THE HERITAGE OF LONGWOOD

When the basement was made livable according to the family's standards of comfort and gracious entertaining, the Nutts moved in. Because of the war and Dr. Nutt's death in 1864, the family was destined never to enjoy a completed Longwood. Descendants of Haller and Julia Nutt nevertheless continued to occupy that lower level for another century.

Five of the original outbuildings at Longwood still exist today. The "Necessary," as the privy was tactfully called, is a square one-story structure located a short distance to the southwest of the mansion.[2] Built in 1860–61, it remains in good condition and is now used by tourists. The kitchen, a one-story frame building with a huge brick fireplace, stands toward the northwest and to the rear of Longwood. The building housing the servants' quarters is also standing, but its interior is in poor condition, as are the carriage house and stables.

Longwood's "Necessary," as it was discretely termed by polite 19th Century society.

The servants' quarters as seen from the roof of the main house. A common Mississippi form of building here in contrast to exotic Longwood.

THE HERITAGE OF LONGWOOD

Around these buildings the grounds of Longwood, once spacious and well tended, today present a picture of desolation. Behind the house, at the family entrance, is "the Circle," a mound of earth with five giant live oak trees growing out of it. According to local legend, "here at sundown every evening a Civil War bride is said to walk with her seven bridesmaids mourning the death of her lost love." [3]

Handsome gardens that once covered fifteen acres are completely overgrown; a full ten acres of these were planted in roses. During the construction period, while the Nutt family was living in the basement, these gardens stretched over so broad an expanse of countryside that supposedly Julia had to travel them by horse and carriage to pick flowers.

On the last page of her book of reprinted material on Longwood, Ina McAdams reproduces a drawing, the "upper part of a framed sketch found in a closet at Longwood." [4] It shows the Longwood gardens in June of 1873, and on the reverse a fancy text tells that the survey was made to locate the dower of Miss Julia A. Nutt. With the octagon house plainly in the center, surrounded by trees and an allée following the drive, the grounds are beautifully laid out. A formal garden is indicated by paths among what must have been the rose bushes.

A letter from Haller Nutt to his wife dated February 12, 1860, speaks of a Mr. Kyle, noting that "Things look well at Longwood, but Mr. Kyle's trees I am afraid will not live ... it may be the very cold weather." The Kyle referred to was Mark Kyle, a gardener or landscape architect sent from Philadelphia to work at Longwood. A bill from him dated May 26, 1860, says, "I will be ready to leave your employ on Monday," as soon as a settlement could be made. Kyle mentions that he worked from October, 1859, "at which date I entered your employ at Longwood." Minus expenses from Philadelphia to Natchez and $57.00, he was due $170.00. Kyle must have stayed on, for another bill dated September 2, 1860, says that he worked for Haller Nutt beginning October 26, 1859. This time he had only $10.00 due. Haller Nutt scribbled figures below the bill, arriving at a total of $164.90, but no further record exists. Un-

War and Aftermath

fortunately, little remains of Kyle's trees and gardens, although some may soon be restored.

While the war raged about him, Haller Nutt continued to operate his plantations. His overseer at Winter Quarters, Hamilton Smith, kept him informed of crops, planting, and maintenance problems. One 1863 project involved gathering cypress floating on the Mississippi River. When the river rose, logs could be floated to the sawmill at Winter Quarters or Evergreen plantation. In April, 1863, Union troops were advancing down the south bank of Lake St. Joseph where Winter Quarters Plantation was located. They were attempting to cross the Mississippi at Bruinsburg Landing. In the process of marching through the countryside, they burned houses, stole food, freed many Negroes, and burned all the cotton they could find. Haller Nutt's plantations were devastated and everything but the main house at Winter Quarters was burned to the ground.[5]

An undated pamphlet published for the Winter Quarters restoration tells Julia Nutt's story of saving the main house at that plantation. According to legend, she hid in a small attic room and overheard General Grant's officers planning their marches. Subsequently, she traveled to the Union camp at Milliken's Bend to plead with General Grant. Grant promised to spare the house, due to Julia's perseverance, if the tale can be believed. However, slave quarters and outbuildings were all burned and livestock and provisions were stolen as the skirmishes between Federal armies and Confederate cavalry continued.[6]

In October, 1863, Haller Nutt began petitioning the Treasury Department of the United States government concerning his losses. He mentioned his Union sympathies and requested permission to purchase and resell cotton.[7] Laws had been passed forbidding cotton speculation by carpetbaggers, but apparently Nutt had hoped to get the exclusive authority to purchase cotton in the area in hopes of recouping his losses. In January, 1864, he went to Vicksburg to try to find labor and probably to try again to obtain the permit to sell cotton. He did get labor in the form of returned slaves, to be paid a minimum wage, but a cotton dealing permit did not come.

On June 15, 1864, Haller Nutt died at the age of forty-eight. Immediately after, Julia issued a terse announcement of the impending funeral services.

Funeral Notice

> The friends and acquaintances of the late HALLER NUTT are invited to attend his funeral, to proceed from his residence on the Woodville Road this (Thursday) evening at 4 1-2 o'clock. Natchez, Thursday morning, June 16, 1864[8]

A physician had given the immediate cause of Dr. Nutt's death as pneumonia; even so, Julia attributed her husband's last illness to the days and weeks during which he had paced the drafty, unfinished stories of Longwood mansion. Her rationalization did not help what thereafter befell the family. Despite his Union sympathies and his anti-secession views, even despite a "protection paper" given him by Union General Ulysses S. Grant, Dr. Nutt's fortune and properties were virtually destroyed.[9] His losses on Louisiana plantations alone were estimated at $1,020,540. He had not only been left penniless, but also the plantation crops, most of the land, and all the farm machinery had been confiscated or burned.

After her husband's death, Julia was responsible for sustaining and educating eight children — with no income from crops, no farm animals, and no money. One of Dr. Nutt's executors held $8,787 in cash that he had to turn over to a Union general. "At this time I had but one week's provisions in my storeroom and no money," Julia recalled later. "I had jewels but I could not sell them; I had dresses but I could not sell them." No one had money, in fact; there was no one to buy. Dr. Nutt's widow continued:

> Then came the dark and winter days of my life. I gathered wild weeds and fed my children on them and when winter came on we thanked God when we could get a little corn. My youngest child was but a baby and my oldest son just sixteen. How we

War and Aftermath

lived, God alone knows.... Many a time and often in years since then have my children gone to bed half starved and we have lived on sour milk. The world did not know what was going on in my private household and therefore it could not pity us.[10]

The main entrance prior to the construction of a new set of stairs.

THE HERITAGE OF LONGWOOD

To add to Mrs. Nutt's troubles, many mechanics' liens were placed against the estate of Haller Nutt, for after the Civil War started, Nutt and many others were desitute. Liens were often secured by merchants to be sure of a valid claim after the war. No one in Natchez could pay bills during this time, but in 1863 Nutt was still buying grandly to furnish the lower floor of Longwood, as many liens indicate. Book NN, page 596, in the Adams County Court House, records one of the more interesting liens on the Nutt estate. Apparently after the death of Haller Nutt, the estate was in such a tangle that Natchez merchants were trying to protect their claims. Among these was the firm of Polkingham and Rarves, sellers of fireplace mantles and other materials, who recorded a lien for supplies they had sold Dr. Nutt. As noted, there are eight fireplace mantles in the basement rooms. There are three of white marble in the bedrooms, a black marble in the hallway (staircase room) and in the parlor, one of oxblood color in the dining room, and one of white marble in what is now the gift shop office. There is an eighth fireplace in what is now the caretaker's kitchen, but it has a wooden mantle. According to family tradition, this room was to have been the children's day nursery.

Julia Nutt tried to reclaim some of their losses by filing suit against the United States government. Julia was not only intelligent, she was also eloquent, as many of the recorded statements in her 1865 deposition testify. Recalling 1863 and 1864, while Dr. Nutt was still alive, Julia's testimony recounted that from "the advent of the Union troops till they all finally left this neighborhood, Longwood was ever open in hospitality to the United States soldier." She commented further that "we once received a large number of wounded and sick soldiers at Longwood and in our large rooms nursed and cared for them. . . . I do not remember a single Union officer who visited Natchez during the war who was not the recipient of the hospitalities of Longwood. [All] received there the welcome and comforts of home. Brig. Gen. M. M. Crocker I nursed through a dangerous illness. To all officers from Gen. Grant down, including Generals Sherman and Logan, Mr. Nutt was known, and known by them as a Union man." [11]

Julia's suit continued year after year as she sought, but never received, full restitution. In time, the U.S. government paid damages approximating $200,000 against claims for assets confiscated or destroyed. The sum did not begin to cover the several million in assets lost in the war, but it did enable Julia to complete the education of the younger children, to hold the family together, and to continue living at Longwood. It was quiet living, compared with what the Nutts had enjoyed while they had their wealth; but they still owned Longwood, whereas others' great estates had been lost due to mortgage foreclosures and other vicissitudes of war and its aftermath.

In her deposition of 1865, Julia completed her testimony by giving a full account of assets lost in the war: $1,530,000 at the hands of the Confederate States; by the United States, in damage to lands and buildings, $100,000; Negroes, $250,000; Dr. Nutt's library, $10,000; paintings, $10,000; and assets which earlier had been listed in claims submitted to both the Commissioner of Claims and the Quartermaster General. Estimated losses: more than $3 million. She assigned no monetary value to her final item: "Life of Haller Nutt, HOW MUCH?" [12]

While Julia was seeking justice from the government, a series of suits and claims were lodged against the estate of Haller Nutt. Distribution of the assets of Dr. Nutt was not accomplished until 1928 and the decree was not recorded until February, 1929. The final decree is noted in Minute Book I, page 218 in the Adams County Court House, Natchez. Cash balance as of July, 1928, was $50,000, which probably represents some of the settlement from the federal government for Mrs. Nutt's claim. The estate may have been kept open in order to pursue the claim against the Federal government, but the heirs were in disagreement over their shares. Appointment of the administrators took a great deal of time. At one point there was even a sale, held March 30, 1868, when Mary Nutt bought the property for $50.00 to keep it in the family.[13] The sale was an effort to satisfy some of the creditors, but an encumbered property was the only asset. While the heirs disagreed over the shares they were to have, there was a suit pending against the federal government and the estate was insolvent. The creditors were never paid and the heirs finally went to the Mississippi supreme court over their shares.

In 1891, Mrs. Nutt must have seen some prosperity, for that spring she solicited three estimates for finishing Longwood.[14] Two letters are from the firm of Lewman & Company in Savannah, Georgia, dated April 14, 1891. The lowest estimate for $6,060.00 was for finishing the first floor, "omitting the Rotunda and main stairs and dressing rooms." This estimate also included a dumbwaiter from the basement to the large drawing room as well as side steps, front steps, and one flight of rear stairs, "but no stairs to the Mound." Lewman's second estimate was for finishing the first floor of the building, "tower complete, second floor hall and one bedroom on the second floor." There were to be blinds for all windows except those on the first floor which were to be installed in glass. This second proposition included, "tower and main stairs and setting nine grates, etc.," for the sum of $8,147.50. The third estimate, longer and more detailed, was from a William R. Kettringham, Natchez, Mississippi, dated April 15, 1891. He was going to do "the entire job, and complete it, that is two floors and Rotunda and all painting, for the sum of $8,850.00." The detailed outline of the work he proposed provides a good look at what remained to be done when the workmen departed. Amidst many detailed specifications, a few items are noteworthy. Kettringham proposed to give all the windows sliding blinds, to finish all the inside doors with hard pine and fit them with brass locks, "with light bronze knobs." The rotunda room would have eight plain glass floor lights, and the other windows were to be of clear glass," except those in the top of the Rotunda — those to be colored glass figured." The rotunda

The central rotunda was to have been splendidly decorated in the manner suggested in Figure 4.

Many of the centering devices for the brick arches are just where the workers left them.

According to family legend, the niches were designed to receive marble statues representing each of the Four Seasons.

niches were to be done in walnut. Kettringham too would install a dumbwater but "up to the top floor where intended at first." All exterior work was included in his estimate, gallery ceilings, painting, and various repairs to the structure. Alas, none of the work was ever done and Longwood still remains unfinished.

In the thirty-three years during which the widow Julia lived at Longwood after her husband's death, her children grew up, most of them married, and moved away. A daughter, also named Julia, did not marry and stayed with her mother at Longwood. One son, Sargent Prentiss, changed his name back to the old spelling — Knut. Educated in Philadelphia and at the University of Virginia, Sargent Prentiss studied law at Natchez before becoming an attorney in Washington, D.C. He "dedicated himself to recuperating the family fortune," and "unaided he prepared the lawsuit against the federal government claiming reparation for the loss and destruction of the family property." [15] With daughter Julia at her side, Julia Nutt lived at Longwood from 1864 until her death in 1897. Miss Julia Nutt lived in the house until 1932 when she died. The last descendants of Haller and Julia Nutt to own Longwood were the five children of Lily Nutt and her husband, James Williams Ward of Washington County, Mississippi — the late Merritt Williams Ward, Robert Julian Ward, James Haller Ward, Julia Ward Blanchard, and Isabelle Ward Pollard.[16]

During many of Longwood's quiet later years, only a bachelor grandson, Merritt Williams Ward, occupied the house. He lived there virtually alone, except for visits from his brother James Haller Ward, till his death in 1939. Children exploring the property invented a story that the wonderful old residence was filled with ghosts and goblins, a tale that imaginative tourists and writers adopted. Another legend also gained currency — that the ghost of Dr. Haller Nutt "paced the empty rooms by day and haunted the grounds by night." [17]

War and Aftermath

NOTES TO CHAPTER 6

1. Hendrix, *The Legend of Longwood*, 23.
2. Pilgrimage Garden Club, "Site of National Significance: Longwood, Mississippi," *Report for the Mississippi Landmarks Commission* (Unpublished report, n.d.), 9.
3. Marshall, Theodora Brinton and Gladys Crail Evans, *A Day in Natchez* (Natchez: The Reliquary, 1946), 98.
4. McAdams, *The Building of Longwood*, 126.
5. Logan, *Mississippi-Louisiana Border Country*, 238.
6. *Ibid.*, 241.
7. *Ibid.*, 239.
8. McAdams, *The Building of Longwood*, 97.
9. Hendrix, *The Legend of Longwood*, 10.
10. McAdams, *The Building of Longwood*, 116.
11. *Ibid.*, 110–18.
12. *Ibid.*, 123–24.
13. Estate of Haller Nutt. Case #1436. File Box 230, Pocket #2. Filed 3-1-1897, Adams County Court House, Natchez, Mississippi.
14. McAdams, *The Building of Longwood*, 98–100.
15. Logan, *Mississippi-Louisiana Border Country*, 242.
16. Merle C. Nutt, *The Nutt Family History* (Phoenix: Merle C. Nutt, 1973), 110.
17. Hendrix, *The Legend of Longwood*, 21.

Chapter 7

Twentieth Century Longwood

In 1968, slightly more than 104 years after the death of Haller Nutt, three of his grandchildren sold Longwood to Mr. and Mrs. Kelly E. McAdams of Austin, Texas. In January, 1970, through the McAdams Foundation, Longwood was deeded over to the Pilgrimage Garden Club of Natchez in order that the structure might be preserved along with other famous Natchez buildings in the club's care. A little more than a year later, on February 14, 1971, ceremonies were held at Longwood to dedicate it as a National Historic Landmark.[1] A bronze plaque commemorating the designation was given to the garden club by the National Park Service of the U.S. Department of the Interior.

The Natchez Pilgrimage Garden Club appointed a committee, headed by physician Dr. Homer A. Whittington to assess the extent of necessary restoration and decide what work needed to be done immediately.[2] The roof, and especially the gutters, were in obvious and severe disrepair. Leakage of water through the substructure had caused extensive damage to some inside timbers. The committee, in searching for the same type of lumber as was used in the original building, found a sizable amount of wood in an old barn that was decaying in the north garden. This supply yielded a number of large timbers that were to be used in rebuilding the long pilasters on the cupola. The barn itself was demolished, providing excellent timbers for restoration of the framework, which had partly rotted. Many galleries, brackets, and columns had also rotted or fallen due to gutter decay and leakage. A start was made at copying and replacing them. Some mouldings, outside gallery ceilings, and gutters were also replaced. Early consideration was given to improving the entrance road. Bottlenecks on the existing narrow roadway had already appeared. An engineer was added to the consulting staff and help from city and county officials was sought in building a fill to replace the small bridge on the present road and another fill across a ditch to provide a parallel road for traffic leaving the property. The committee also recommended that the city be urged to bring water mains to the property, not only to assist in maintenance of the grounds, but also for protection in case of fire.

In preparation for the 1971 dedication program, priority was given to flooring and finishing the front porch of Longwood, which was to be used as a stage for the ceremonies. Carpenters repaired flooring that was giving way on the structure's northwest side. The understructure was found to be badly deteriorated, so a concrete base was poured on which a new floor was laid.

In repairing the house structure, balconies, and porches, the committee tried to assure that restoration work would conform to the original design. Much work proceeded in accordance with the specifications made out by Samuel Sloan (see Appendix). Literature and early photographs of the house provided additional guidance. The committee members found an original watercolor painting of Longwood probably made by Sloan or his staff. The ceiling of the upper porch on the west side of the building, which had never been completed, was finished with the other three verandas serving as models. The porches were then painted.

A nationally known retail firm provided paint free of charge and sent an expert from Chicago to advise on painting procedures.[3] The Pilgrimage Garden Club supplied the funds with which to pay the salaries of the painters and other costs of restoration. These funds were derived to a large extent from admissions paid by visitors to the house. Time and weather had

Watercolor of Longwood as finished. Reputedly done by Samuel Sloan or a member of his firm. The picture is now located at Saragossa Plantation, Natchez.

worked against the original paint applied to the building. Much of it had to be scraped off before new coats could be put on; in some places, as many as three layers were removed. Also, much of the old wood was found to stain new paint, so that special undercoatings had to be used.

The painters and technicians on the job encountered other problems in the repainting of Longwood. The building's exterior trim was in the process of being covered with a lead and oil coating at the time all work ceased on the building in mid-1861. This covering did not fare well on those portions of the house that caught the brunt of weather conditions. Areas exposed to open weather, such as the veranda and balcony balustrades and columns, were bare of paint by 1971 when the technicians arrived for an inspection. The sides that faced away from the weather were, however, found to be coated with the remains of the original lead and oil product.[4] All the woodwork was treated and painted carefully. The architect had specified light paint, white lead, and linseed oil boiled, and noted that "the exterior woodwork such as cornices, verandas, cupola, etc., will receive four coats of paint and two of sand of tint corresponding to the color of the walls."[5] The new white may be a bit bright, but it will protect the woodwork for many generations even if it does emphasize the cut-out work details beyond Sloan's intentions.

Clearly the architect wanted the structure to be all one color. The shade of the exterior walls was specified by Sloan to represent "Picton" Stone. In his *Homestead Architecture*, Sloan described this stone: "We should not neglect to notice the stone imported from Nova Scotia, known under the name of 'Pictou,' or Acadia freestone. Lately this stone has been extensively used in the vicinity of Philadelphia, and, aside from its delightful shade of color, it is recommended as a durable material."[6] Precisely what the color of "Picton" stone is, or what exact color Sloan had in mind, is still being debated. Henry W. Krotzer, Jr., of the New Orleans restoration firm of Koch and Wilson, consultants of the Pilgrimage Garden Club, wrote:

Twentieth Century Longwood

We by no means suggest painting the building as originally intended. However, we do think that the building would be greatly enhanced if the millwork and sheet metal were painted a color that blends in with the brick — a pinkish or reddish tan mixed with sand. The white exaggerates the millwork details and overstates their importance; the aluminum paint on the dome (is was black in the 1920s) is not very handsome.

Practical considerations surely do not call for undertaking such a painting job now, when so much has just been done. However, with scaffolding in place, would it be advisable to paint the top of the building now? I think specifically of the dome and possibly the lantern. Later on, the lower portions of the building could be painted the new color.[7]

Mr. Krotzer also noted that "the visual effect was to be that of a building constructed entirely of stone, as Moorish buildings were." Someday the outside walls will be so painted, when the garden club has the funds.

Recent restoration has been concerned with preserving the fabric of the building. Under the able direction of Dix Fowler of Natchez, Longwood has been stabilized in such a manner from within so that it should last another 140 years. Beginning in November, 1973, Fowler's restoration was guided by Samuel Sloan's original specifications and the original work. Many of the windows which had been boarded up were redone with original materials. Rotted gutters were replaced and missing woodwork was restored to original patterns. Architectural detail was carefully copied and replaced as were the fasciae and mouldings below the dome. The clerestory window coverings were repaired and fixed so they can now be opened. Sixteen pilasters on the clerestory level were carefully copied from the original and were fitted into place. Water seepage which had damaged the interior over the years was stopped by sealing with modern compounds and new runoffs were devised where needed.

The interior of the house was in remarkably good condition due to the fact that many openings had never been sealed. Inside, the wood was in good shape for, in Fowler's words, the building had been "able to breathe all these years" and the wood did not rot. Unfortunately, these same openings had admitted pigeons, creating quite a mess as well as a health hazard. The flapping of wings in dark recesses of the cupola and the soft cooing of the birds have created a suitable atmosphere for the ghost of Haller Nutt legends. Snakes would come in at the base of the house searching for pigeon eggs and often worked their way to the upper stories, only to fall on unsuspecting tourists with terrifying effect. To keep the pigeons out, hardware cloth, similar to a fine mesh chicken wire, was installed over the large arched openings. As this is inconspicuously installed, most people do not even notice it. Snakes were kept out by sealing the foundation of the structure. Today the building still breathes, but the pests are eliminated.

Work remains to be done on the base of the dome and there are tentative plans to replace the spire–flagpole. Despite the fact that the shaft was destroyed by woodpeckers, much of the carving and moulding remains. With existent photographs of the spire, it could easily be restored. It has been suggested that a helicopter, with widespread publicity, should put a spire in place again.[8]

All who have worked on Longwood in the preservation process have expressed great admiration for the craftsmanship of the builders. Beautifully mitered joints, visible today, are testimony to the German–Dutch carpenters sent by Sloan to do the construction. Most of the architectural detail was cut and fitted together in Philadelphia and shipped to the site to be placed on the building. Samuel Sloan must have overseen this work. The exterior carpentry detail is astounding; all joints are perfectly fitted.

Working with original specifications and following extant parts carefully, the modern restoration of Longwood has been able to stabilize this wonderful building, which is not only unusual in style but also in construction. Longwood is a builder's monument, as well as a mansion of architectural and cultural importance.

There are numerous conclusions about the significance of

The overgrown gardens with Spanish moss hanging from the trees seemed to engulf Longwood prior to the grounds being cleared by the Pilgrimage Garden Club. This photograph *circa* 1932 shows the house in its most romantic mood.

Longwood seems removed from reality. Its dark interior and bright, ornate balconies contrast with the encroaching trees laden with Spanish moss.

At the rear entrance to Longwood is a mound with a circle of five giant live oak trees growing on it. At sundown each evening a Civil War bride is supposed to be seen walking with seven bridesmaids to mourn the death of a lost love.

Longwood. Writing for *The Journal of the Society of Architectural Historians,* George L. Hersey said of Samuel Sloan and another architect of the Civil War period, Isaac H. Hobbs, Jr.:

> These men ... conducted a series of sometimes wild and sometimes highly ingenious experiments with the architectural principles of their day in the form of complex, rather sophisticated variations on the classic American farmhouse arrangement. These experiments helped to liberate the thinking of the American householder and do away with the 18th Century and Greek Revival formalism. The plans of the "Lady's Book" houses prepared the way for the wide-open plans of Late Victorian times, and similar freedom in elevational treatments ... especially room forms ... have done much to prepare the public for the Shingle Style and early modern houses.[9]

One such design was, of course, Sloan's "Oriental villa," as described in *Godey's Lady's Magazine.* Dr. Nutt himself felt that this design, as exemplified in Longwood, would become a trend-setting form. "It is creating much admiration," he wrote in 1861, reiterating, "I think after this the octagon will be the style." [10]

Margaret Hendrix, former custodian of Longwood, has provided another view. When asked by tourists, "Why not complete construction?" she has commented succinctly, "No, leave it as a monument to the heart-rending break of the Civil War. Let it mark the end of an era." [11]

A prospectus nominating Longwood as a national historical site comments, "the largest and most elaborate of the octagon houses built in the United States, Longwood also is one of the finest surviving examples of an Oriental Revival residence, illustrating the exotic phase of architectural romanticism that flourished in mid-19th century America." [12]

A single paragraph was devoted to Longwood in *A Guide to Early American Homes — South,* published in 1956. "Under construction during the Civil War but never completed," the item read, "it is a weird, five-story structure dominated by a great fat cupola. Only the first floor was finished and the house is not lived in. A curiosity." [13] Clay Lancaster, author of

Twentieth Century Longwood

Architectural Follies in America, cited Longwood in his book, believing the structure qualified as a "folly" on three counts: (1) it was never finished; (2) it was of a bizarre oriental style, and (3) it had an odd shape. He softens his indictment, however: "Its windows boarded up and the house abandoned, it now stands in mute testimony of a flourishing culture that was obliterated by civil strife. The tropical jungle closes in. The live-oak trees are draped in long streamers of Spanish moss; no festive decorations, these, but the tattered and shredded garments worn by a great estate that has seen better days and fell short of attaining the full measure of its grandeur." [14]

The people of today's Natchez, basing their opinions more on sentiment than on architectural history, look at Longwood from the memory-laden point of view of the family that built it. In her pamphlet called *Legend of Longwood,* Margaret Hendrix expresses the Natchez point of view: "This, then, is Longwood, a man's dream of grandeur and gracious living, un-

Stereopticon photograph *circa* 1900. Note boarded-up basement, ladder to first story, and the 25-foot spire still intact.

THE HERITAGE OF LONGWOOD

finished . . . but forever unforgettable. The story of Longwood is a story of love, for much love and many people have passed through the pages of its history." [15] Mrs. Hendrix freely admits that her booklet on Longwood "reeks of sentiment," but adds, "that is the feeling and outlook of most of us old-timers." She goes on to say how she believes that many tourists enjoy the "pathos and romance" of the unusual old home.

> My personal memories of Longwood span over fifty years of happenings of every description including not only births and deaths but christenings, weddings, receptions and picnics and parties galore. For this reason I am always distressed when some visitors spend a few days prowling around Longwood and depart to write their own "facts and figures" often picturing the place as unlived in and abandoned.
>
> To me one of the remarkable things about Longwood is the fact that although it is incomplete and unfinished with 4/5 hollow, bare and shell-like floors rising above its ground floor basement, for over 100 years it has been and remains essentially a *home*. Surely no other structure its equal boasts such a history in this country. For this reason I deplore the writers who give the book-reading public and potential visitor the impression of a totally derelict building.[16]

Trend-setter? Memento? Oddity? The questions remain. Perhaps Longwood might truly have been a trend-setting first, as Dr. Nutt believed it would be, had not the Civil War effectively brought to an end the development of this kind of southern architecture. But Longwood stands today as a remembrance, a reminder of a gracious way of life that was obliterated, never to return. As for its being an oddity, Longwood Villa represents a fabulous, authentic, and beloved example of architectural innovation — if not of architectural folly.

The greatest of the "ghosts along the Mississippi" stands witness to the cotton fortune of Dr. Haller Nutt and his desire for a house beyond all houses. It is too easy, however, to sneer at the Byzantine dome, Venetian balconies, and Moorish arches. Longwood indicates a very particular nineteenth-century architectural mentality. American architecture was never really able to make up its mind — should we go our own way with in-

According to Natchez stories, the ghost of Haller Nutt still paces these rooms in a suitable atmosphere for the tragedy of unfinished Longwood.

novative plans, as with Sloan's creative adaptation of Fowler's octagon, or should we import style and cover ourselves with exotic ornament? Elaboration for its own sake as a display of wealth was a favorite American goal. Take forms from any context and rearrange. When in doubt cover with ornament. John Burchard and Albert Bush-Brown in *The Architecture of America* sum up the nineteenth-century viewpoint seen at Longwood, as well as bringing it up to date, when they remark about this type of style: "It was a sincere, if inept, search for something good looking, no less sincere than the flight to streamlining three quarters of a century later." [17]

NOTES TO CHAPTER 7

1. "Longwood Dedication as Historic Landmark Will Be February 14," *Jackson Daily News*, January 17, 1971, Section D, 14.
2. Homer A. Whittington, "Progress Report to the Executive Board of the Pilgrimage Garden Club," n.d., 1.
3. "Longwood," pamphlet issued by The Pilgrimage Garden Club, Natchez, Mississippi, 3.
4. A. H. Migdal, Memorandum to H. L. Beeferman, De Soto, Inc., Des Plaines, Illinois, "Inspection for 'Longwood' for Exterior Painting Recommendations," March 2, 1971.
5. McAdams, *The Building of Longwood*, 46.
6. Sloan, *Sloan's Homestead Architecture*, 33.
7. Letter from Mr. Henry W. Krotzer, Jr., to Mrs. Hyde Jenkins, president, The Natchez Pilgrimage Garden Club, May 23, 1973.
8. *Ibid.*
9. Hersey, "Godey's Choice," 110.
10. McAdams, *The Building of Longwood*, 24.
11. Margaret Shields Hendrix, conversation with the author, August, 1969.
12. Pilgrimage Garden Club, "Site of National Significance," 1.
13. Dorothy Pratt and Richard Pratt, *A Guide to Early American Homes — South* (New York: Bonanza Books, 1965, 140.
14. Clay Lancaster, *Architectural Follies in America* (Rutland, Vt. and Tokyo, Japan: Charles E. Tuttle Company, 1960), 101.
15. Hendrix, *The Legend of Longwood*, 9 ff.
16. Letter to author from Margaret Shields Hendrix, December 28, 1974.
17. John Burchard and Albert Bush-Brown, *The Architecture of America* (Boston: Little, Brown, 1961), 100.

Appendix

Specifications
(McAdams' transcription)

Of the workmanship and materials required in the erection and completion of a residence for Haller Nutt, Esq., Natchez, Mississippi.

GENERAL DESCRIPTION

The ground plan of the building will be octagonal in outline — the central part or rotunda will also be octagonal and 24'0" in diameter, surrounded by galleries on each story above the first and lighted from a cupola above the main roof of the building — this being sixteen-sided is pierced with a corresponding number of windows and is surmounted by a bulbiform dome.

The main or central portion of the building is three stories in height; from the alternate sides of the octagon project wings of two stories in height; with two-story verandas of twelve feet in width occupying the interspaces. Beneath the whole building is a Basement provided with spacious areas for light and ventilation. The height of the several stories is as follows:

Basement	9'0" in the clear
Principal story	14'0" in the clear
Second story	12'0" in the clear
Third story	9'0" in the clear

The arrangement of the various apartments is clearly set forth by the ground plans, upon which the names and dimensions of the same are marked and figured, while the external finish is represented by the Elevation and details.

EXCAVATIONS

Excavations will be made to such depth as may be required so that the basement shall be nine feet in the clear of the floor and ceiling, and trenches prepared for the reception of the walls of such depth below the level of the basement floor as may be adjudged sufficient to give a permanent foundation. All the earth not required for grading purposes to be removed and deposited as directed.

APPENDIX

BRICK WORK

All the exterior walls of the building and all the interior walls with the exception of a few minor divisions tinted on the drawing to represent wood will be built of brick of suitable quality, and well laid in mortar composed of about two parts of sharp sand to one of fresh lime. The fireplaces are all so arranged that the flues from them will vent into vertical circular shafts at a proper height to receive the best draughts. These shafts are four in number and their position and that of the fireplaces with relation to them as shown on the plans; they must be well parquetted throughout their whole height to extend above the roof and each capped with a single stone moulded as per detail drawing and properly set. The exterior walls will be built with a space between the inner and the outer sections as shown by the ground plans—and to obviate the effects of capillary attraction a course of slate will be laid in the wall extending through its entire thickness at the height of a few inches above the surface of the ground. The mortar will be removed from the joint of the exterior walls to the depth of half an inch to insure the adhesion of the rough-casting.

All area walls, piers for the verandas, and a furnace chamber in the basement to be built as per plan. All bricks coming in contact with the earth in the foundation and all used in paving the areas to be hard-burnt—the latter to be smooth—selected for the purpose.

CARPENTER WORK

The joists for the first and second floors and corresponding verandas and galleries will be 3" x 10"—those for the third floor will be 3" x 10"—those for the upper galleries will be 3" x 9"—the ceiling joists throughout 3" x 8" and the studding required for the wood partitions 3" x 4" and all placed 16" between centres. All the joists will be straightened and solidly bedded in the walls on the whole surface of their bearings and each tier exceeding twelve feet in length will have a course of lattice bridging through the centre. The studding in partitions will be set edgewise for greater strength and securely fastened to the floor and ceiling. The rafters will all be 3" x 5" placed two feet apart, supported at the bottom on a raising plate secured to the ceiling joists and at the top on the division walls and boarded over for metal covering.

The cupola will be framed with posts of 5" x 7" scantling extending from the third floor to the height represented by the drawing—the plate will be formed of two thicknesses of 3" joists pinned together so as to break joints. The framing of the dome will be in accordance with the drawings and secured where necessary with one-inch iron

APPENDIX

bolts and the necessary straps. All trimmers for stairs and fireplaces will be double, pinned together and well framed and keyed.

FLOORS

The floors will all be laid with 5/4" heart-pine, mill-worked and well-seasoned boards, securely nailed to the joists and afterwards smoothed off. The veranda floor will be smoothed on the underside and the joints beaded—the joists and plates will also be smoothed and moulded on the lower edge. The ceiling of the second story of the verandas will be laid with boards as above described with the smooth side downwards and the joints beaded. The floors of the Hall adjoining Veranda and the Rotunda in the Basement and Hall and veranda on the first story will be laid with marble filings; that of the Rotunda in the Principal story will be laid with Encaustic Tiles of ornamental pattern having floor lights arranged to harmonize with the general effect for the purpose of lighting the apartment beneath. The remainder of the basement floor will be laid with slate on a bed of concrete.

STAIRS

A flight of Geometrical Stairs will be constructed in the Front Hall—the step boards of these will be 5/4" thick, the risers 1" thick, tongued, glued and blocked together and let into the wall string. And supported on strong carriages. The hand-rail and newel will be of black walnut, and the balusters of light-colored wood and all properly proportioned to the magnitude of the stairs as laid down on the plan.

A flight of stairs on the rear veranda from the Basement to the second floor and one within the main building from the second to the third floor and also a small flight from the third floor to the gallery above will be constructed as represented by the drawings.

The galleries will be finished with balusters and railing of neat pattern to correspond with the style of the stair-railing.

WINDOWS

All the windows will be made for sash 1 3/4" thick, double hung with the best-patent cord, weights and sham—axle pullies. Those opening to the verandas on the first floor extend entirely to the floor—all opening to the Balconies and all on the second floor will not reach the floor by six inches. All on both first and second stories will have outside pivot blinds arranged to slide into the walls or sheaves made for the purpose. The windows of the third story will have inside shutters made to fold against the jambs and hung with the usual hinges and back flaps and secured with proper fastenings.

APPENDIX

DOORS

All the doors opening to the veranda will be 2½" thick made folding, hung with 4" x 4" butts and secured with an eight-inch mortice rebate lock and two iron plate flush bolts to each. The sliding doors opening from the rotunda will also be 2½" thick and to move on 6" sheaves with brass ways—to be secured with the proper sliding door locks.

All the doors in the basement, all the communicating doors on the first and second floors will be 2" thick. All the doors on the third story and all the closet doors on the second story will be 1½". All the 2" doors will be hung with 4" x 4" butts and the 1½" doors will be hung with 3½" x 3½" butts. These doors will all be secured with mortise locks and those that are folding will require mortise rebate locks and flush bolts.

The material for the doors throughout will be white pine excepting only those of the principal story which will be walnut.

The door frames will be made of 4" x 9" plank; those in the basement with square, and those on the principal floor with semi-circular heads—the jamb-casing of the inside doors will be 2" thick with rebate straps nailed on.

The exterior finish such as cornices, balconies and verandas, including the cupola, are to be finished after the detail drawings numbered as in the following schedule:

No. 4: Details of Balconies;
No. 5: Details of Porches;
No. 6: Deails of Cupola.

INSIDE DRESSINGS

All dressings of the doors and windows on the first floor will be 8" wide, all on the second floor will be 6" wide and those in the basement and third story will be 4" wide. The wash-boards in the first story will be 12" wide, including a sub and moulding of 3" each; those on the second will be 10" wide including a sub and moulding of 2½" each; those in the Basement and third story will be 8" wide, with a sub and moulding of 2" each. The dressings of the window and door will be neatly moulded the outer moulding of the dressing to member with the top-moulding of the wash-board.

The closets will be filled up and shelved as may be directed, as also the Bath and Clothes rooms.

ROOFING

The roof will be overlaid with one cross leaded roofing tin, painted

APPENDIX

on both sides, the upper side to have two coats. The dome will be covered with sheet lead properly secured and ribbed as represented by the drawing. All the gutters to be formed so as to convey the water to eight-inch conductors placed at the intersection of the verandas with the wings—these will be iron and connect with a pipe leading to the cistern placed over the kitchen.

PLASTERING AND FRESCOING

All the walls and ceilings throughout including the dome will be plastered with two coats of brown mortar and one of white, hard finish. Cornices will be run in the angles of all the principal rooms both first and second story in accordance with the drawings given for the same. Centre pieces of proper proportions, and ornamental pattern will be placed in the ceilings of all the principal rooms. The mortar for the plastering to be composed of clean sharp sand and fresh lime properly proportioned and well mixed with slaughtered hair. All lath to be sound and free from bark.

The walls and dome of the rotunda as also the walls and ceilings of such rooms as may be directed by the proprietors to be frescoed to correspond with the general style of the interior finish of the building.

ROUGH-CASTING

All the exterior walls of the building will be rough cast in the best manner by a person familiar with the business. The sand for the purpose being washed and mixed with lime in proper proportions. All angles and washes to be properly formed and the whole surface tinted to represent Picton Stone.

PAINTING AND GLAZING

All the woodwork that it is usual to paint will receive three coats of white lead and linseed oil boiled. The exterior woodwork such as cornices, verandas, cupola etc. will receive four coats of paint and two of sand of tint corresponding to the color of the walls. All the walnut doors, interior hand-rails, newel and balusters and such work as may be grained will receive three coats of best varnish. The washboards, dressings, doors, sash, etc. throughout will be painted such tint as may be directed.

All the glass in the first story will be French plate and all the remainder the best American, well bedded, bradded and buck-puttied.

PLUMBING AND GAS-FITTING

All the water from the roof is to be conveyed beneath the ground,

APPENDIX

to an iron cistern in the kitchen, above the level of the bath-room, from which the bath-tub and wash-basin adjacent will be supplied. The bath-tub will be paneled front, neatly filled up and lined with copper-tinned and planished.

The wash-basin will have a counter-sunk marble top with door beneath. All the fixtures will be silver-plated.

Pipes will be concealed in the walls of sufficient capacity for the introduction of gas for the lighting of all the rooms. All the rooms on the first story will have drop-lights and all the others, side-lights.

BELLS, SAFE, LIGHTNING-ROD AND GRATES, ETC.

The front door and each of the principal rooms will have a bell placed beneath the rear veranda. A speaking tube of approved patent will extend from dining room to kitchen. A safe will be provided in the large family room first story for the reception of silverware.

A lightning rod will be put up to extend above the finial of dome and properly secured and planted in the ground.

Grates of modern style will be required to each of the fire-places as presented on the plan.

A furnace to be placed in the basement Hall for warming the Hall and Rotunda in each story properly set with a brick chamber and the necessary flues and registers.

Pipe for hanging pictures will be arranged in the several rooms as directed.

MANTLES

Marble mantles of neat and approved pattern will be set to each fire-place as represented on the drawings.

HARDWARE AND IRONWORK

All the hardware described under the head of carpentry and all such other hardware as may be necessary to complete the building in all its parts will be required of a good and approved quality.

The hinges and the knobs in the first story and the bell-pull at front door will all be silver-plated—the remainder of the knobs throughout to be white porcelain. An iron railing in front of verandas will be required to enclose the areas, of neat and approved pattern. Also, such bolts, anchors, straps, and jambscrews as may be required will be furnished of proper dimensions and quality.

Bibliography

Ames, Kenneth. "George Henkels, Nineteenth-Century Philadelphia Cabinetmaker." *Antiques* (October, 1973), 641–650.

Andrews, Wayne. *Architecture, Ambitions, and Americans.* New York: Harper and Brothers, 1955. (Rev. ed.)

Bettersworth, John K. *Confederate Mississippi.* Baton Rouge: Louisiana State University Press, 1943.

Bibliographical and Historical Memoirs of Mississippi, Vol. II. Chicago: The Goodspeed Publishing Company, 1891.

Burchard, John and Albert Bush-Brown. *The Architecture of America.* Boston, Massachusetts: Little, Brown, 1961.

Claiborne, J. F. H. *Mississippi.* Jackson, Mississippi: Power and Bardsdale, Publishers, 1880.

Cooledge, Harold N., Jr. "A Sloan Checklist." *Journal of the Society of Architectural Historians,* 19 (March, 1960), 34–38.

Cooper, J. Wesley. *Ante-Bellum Houses of Natchez.* Natchez: Southern Historical Publications, Inc., 1970.

Coulter, E. Merton. "Commercial Intercourse with the Confederacy in The Mississippi Valley, 1861–1865." *The Mississippi Valley Historical Review,* (March, 1919), 277-395.

Duke University, Perkins Library, Manuscript Department, Durham, North Carolina. Haller Nutt Collection.

Duval, Mary V. *History of Mississippi.* Louisville, Kentucky: Courier–Journal Printing Company, 1887.

Fitch, James Marston. *American Building I: The Historical Forces That Shaped It.* Boston: Houghton Mifflin Company, and Cambridge: The Riverside Press, 1966.

Fowler, O. S. *A Home for All, Or the Gravel Wall and Octagon Mode of Building.* New York: Fowler and Wells, Publishers, 1853.

Fulkerson, H. S. *Early Days in Mississippi.* Baton Rouge: Otto Claitor, Publishers, 1937.

Godey's Lady's Book, LXII, Philadelphia, 1861.

Gresham, Matilda. *Life of Walter Quintin Gresham.* Vol. I. Chicago: Rand McNally & Company, 1919.

BIBLIOGRAPHY

Henderson, Margaret Shields. *The Legend of Longwood.* Natchez: Hudson Printing Company, 1972.

Hersey, George L. "Godey's Choice," *Journal of the Society of Architectural Historians,* 18 (October, 1959), 104–111.

Hitchcock, Henry-Russell. *The Pelican History of Art: Architecture, 19th and 20th Centuries.* Middlesex, England; Baltimore, Md.; and Victoria, Australia: Penguin Books, 1969. (Rev. ed.)

Huntington Library, San Marino, California. Archives. Sloan-Nutt Letter File.

James, D. Clayton. *Antebellum Natchez.* Baton Rouge: Louisiana State University Press, 1968.

Kane, Harnett T. *Natchez on the Mississippi.* New York: Bonanza Books, 1967.

Lancaster, Clay. *Architectural Follies in America.* Rutland, Vt., and Tokyo, Japan: Charles E. Tuttle Company, 1960.

Logan, Marie T. *Mississippi-Louisiana Border Country: A History of Rodney, Mississippi, St. Joseph, Louisiana, and Environs.* Baton Rouge: Claitor's Publishing Division, 1970.

"Longwood Dedication Will Be February 14." *Jackson Daily News,* January 17, 1971, Section D, p. 14.

"Longwood." Pamphlet issued by The Pilgrimage Garden Club, Natchez, Mississippi. Natchez: Pilgrimage Garden Club, n.d.

Lord, Walter (ed.). *The Freemantle Diary: The South at War:* Boston: Little, Brown, and Company in cooperation with Bantam Books, 1954.

Lowery, Robert and William McGardle. *A History of Mississippi.* Jackson, Mississippi: R. H. Henry and Company, 1891.

Maass, John. *The Gingerbread Age, a View of Victorian America.* New York: Bramhall House, 1957.

Marshall, Theodora Britton, and Gladys Crail Evans. *A Day in Natchez.* Natchez: The Reliquary, 1946.

———. *They Found It in Natchez.* New Orleans: Pelican Publishing Company, 1940.

McAdams, Ina May Ogletree. *The Building of Longwood.* Austin: Private Publication, 1972.

Migdal, A. H. Memorandum to H. L. Beeferman, De Soto, Inc., Des Plaines, Illinois. "Inspection of 'Longwood' for Exterior Painting Recommendations," March 2, 1971.

Moore, John Hebron. *Andrew Brown and Cypress Lumbering in the Old Southwest.* Baton Rouge: Louisiana State University Press, 1967.

Murray, Elizabeth Dunbar. *My Mother Used to Say.* Boston: The Christopher Publishing House, 1959.

BIBLIOGRAPHY

Nutt, Merle C. *The Nutt Family Through the Years 1635–1973*. Phoenix: Merle C. Nutt, 1973.

Oliver, Nola Nance. *This Too is Natchez*. New York: Hastings House, Inc., 1953.

Pilgrimage Garden Club, "Site of National Significance: Longwood, Mississippi," *Report for the Mississippi Landmarks Commission* (Unpublished report, n.d.).

Pishel, Robert Gordon. *Natchez—Museum City of the Old South*. Tulsa, Oklahoma: Magnolia Publishing Company, 1959.

Pratt, Dorothy and Richard Pratt. *A Guide to Early American Homes—South*. New York: Bonanza Books, Inc., 1956.

Sloan, Samuel. *Sloan's Homestead Architecture*. Philadelphia: J. B. Lippincott and Company, 1861.

―――――. *The Model Architect*. Philadelphia: E. S. Jones and Company, 1852.

―――――. "Villa in the Oriental Style." *Godey's Lady's Book and Magazine*, LXII (January, 1961), 87–88.

Smith, Reid and John Owens. *The Majesty of Natchez*. Montgomery, Alabama: Paddle Wheel Publications, Inc., 1969.

Tyree, Mrs. Raymond (comp.). *Natchez Antebellum Homes*. Natchez: Tom L. Ketchings Company, 1964.

U.S. Federal Writers Project. *Mississippi: A Guide to the Magnolia State*. New York: Hastings House, 1939.

Van Court, Catherine. *In Old Natchez*. New York: Doubleday, Doran and Company, 1938.

Whittington, Homer A. "Progress Report to the Executive Board of the Pilgrimage Garden Club," n.d.

Whitwell, William L. "Longwood—A Remembrance of Eastern Magnificence." "*Hollins College Bulletin*, XXI (February, 1971), 2–5.

Williams, Henry L., and Ottalie K. Williams. *A Guide to Old American Houses*. New York: A. S. Barnes, 1962.

Winter Quarters. Pamphlet. Private Publication, n.d.

Index

Adams County, Mississippi: acreage owned in, 23
Adams County Court House, Natchez, Mississippi, 26n, 76, 77
American Institute of Architects, Philadelphia Chapter, 13
Andrews and Son, 13
An Essay on Household Furniture, 60
Araby Plantation, Louisiana, 22, 25, 27n
Architectural Review and American Builder's Journal, 13
Ashburn, estate in Natchez, Mississippi, 23

Baltimore, Maryland, 13
Basement, 50, 69
Bedrooms (Chambers), 50
Berwick, England, 19
Bills of Lading, 52
Blanchard, Julia Ward, 80
Blockade (of southern ports), 64
Bricks: manufacture at site, 16, 51, cost of, 50
Brown, Andrew: sawmill, 51

Caldwell (Philadelphia Jeweler), 12
Canada: Nutt's trip to, 12
Carpenters, 88
Chapel Hill College, North Carolina, 19
Chestnut Street, Philadelphia, Pennsylvania, 67
Cistern, 50
City Hotel, 13
Closets, 69
Cloverdale Plantation, Natchez, Mississippi, 27n
Cnut (early spelling for Nutt), 19
Costs, 47, 50
County Kent, England, 19
Crocker, Brig. General M. M., 76
Cumming and Brodie, 52

Dedication Program, 1971, 84
Dimensions, of building, 50, 51
Domesday Book, 19
Donegana Hotel, 12
Dumbwaiter, 80
Dunbar: family mentioned, 66

England: as source of tile, 59
Estimates: to finish house, 78, 79
Evergreen Plantation, Louisiana, 22, 27n, 73

Fireplaces: placement, 50; projected and present, 69; today, 76
Fireplace Venting System, 50
Fishkill, New York, 12
Fowler, Dix, 87
Fowler, Orson S.: theories, 12; octagon form of, 29, 31; on the kitchen, 31
Furniture: order cards for, 60; dining room, 61; library, 61; parlor, 61; Samuel Sloan sending, 64; present piano, 65

Gardens, 72
Godey's Lady's Book: description of, 13; plan for Longwood mentioned, 92
Grant, General Ulysses S., 73, 74, 77
Greble, Edwin, 52
Gresham, General Walter Quintin, 26
Gresham, Matilda, 26, 64

Hard Times Landing, Mississippi, 23
Harrison, S. A., 59
Hendrix, Margaret, 92, 93, 94
Henkels, George: cabinetmaker, 60; furniture of, 61, 66, 67
Hobbs, Isaac H., Jr., 92

Jefferson County, Mississippi, 19, 27n

INDEX

Ker, Eliza, 19
Ker, Judge David, 19
Kettringham, William R., 78
Kitchen, 70
Knut (early spelling of Nutt), 19
Knut, Sargeant Prentiss, 80
Knutt, Thomas, 19
Knutt, William, 19
Koch and Wilson, 86
Krotzer, Henry W., Jr., 86, 87
Kyle, Mark, 72, 73

Lake George, New York, 12
Laurel Hill Plantation, 27n
Lewman & Company, 78
Lime: shipment of, 52
Lincoln, Abraham, 64, 65
Lippincott, J. P. & Co., 16
Lithograph: of Longwood, 57
Logan, General, 77
London, England, 19

McAdams Foundation, 83
McAdams, Mr. & Mrs. Kelly E., 83
Madame Chegary's and d'Hervilly's Boarding and Day School for Young Ladies, 12
Mirrors: proposed use of, 11
Montreal, Canada, 12

National Park Service, U. S. Department of the Interior, 83
New Orleans, Louisiana: transfer of materials, 52; blockade of, 64; source of present piano, 65
New York City, 12
New York State, 12
Nova Scotia: stone from, 86
Nutt, Austin, 25
Nutt, Calvin R., 25
Nutt, Carrie Routh, 25, 26
Nutt, Fanny, Smith, 25
Nutt, Dr. Haller: inspiration for house, 5; trip to northeast, 12; taste, 14; relations with Samuel Sloan, 14, 15; letters to Samuel Sloan, 16, 17, 18; son of Elisa and Rush, 19; education of, 22; slaves of, 25; family of, 25; destruction of his property, 25; petition to U. S. Government, 73; death of, 74; losses after war, 74; estate of, 76, 77, 78

Nutt, Haller, Jr., 25
Nutt, John Ker, 25
Nutt, Julia Augusta (Miss), 25, 72, 80
Nutt, Julia (Mrs. Haller): trip to northeast, 12; taste, 14; story about new home at Longwood, 23; children of, 25; saving Winter Quarters, 73; after husband's death, 74, 75; suit against U. S. Government, 76, 77
Nutt, Lily, 25, 80
Nutt, Mary, 78
Nutt, Mary Ella, 25
Nutt, Rittenhouse, 19
Nutt, Rushworth (Dr. Rush), 19
Nutt, Sargeant Prentiss (Knutt), 25, 80

Octagon: as a house type, 12
"Oriental Villa": style and description, 4, 5

Philadelphia, Pennsylvania: material costs at, 5; Nutt's trip to, 12, 13; artisans and masons from, 16; on Samuel Sloan's stationery, 16; Dr. Rush Nutt studying in, 19; brick layers from, 51; source of materials, 51, 52; stone source, 52; Watson lithograph, 57; source of furniture, 60; landscape architect from, 72
Philadelphia Exhibition 1876, 13
Picton stone, 52, 86
Pilgrimage Garden Club, 66, 83, 84, 86
Pipes: water and gas, 50
Polkingham and Rarves, 76
Pollard, Isabelle Ward, 80
Porter, Charles, 18n
Privy, 70

Quebec, Canada, 12

Raleigh, North Carolina: governor's mansion, 13
Repainting (20th Century), 84, 86
Room, William L., 18n
Rooms (dimensions), 47
Rosalie, Natchez, Mississippi, 26
Routh, Job, 26n
Rush, Dr. Benjamin, 19

St. Nicholas Hotel, 12
Saratoga Springs, New York, 12

INDEX

Savannah, Georgia, 78
Schartz, Oliver, 18n
Servants' Quarters, 43, 70
Sherman, General, 77
Sloan, Samuel: style description of "Oriental Villa", 4; first contact with the Nutts, 12; designs for *Godey's Lady's Book,* 13; relations with Haller Nutt, 14, 15; stationery, 16; "Oriental Villa" design, 29; on the adaptation of ancient designs and styles, 36, 39; on the choice of the "Oriental Villa" style, 41; on walls, 41; trips to Natchez, Mississippi, 43; material shipments, 52; as a tastemaker, 60; on the antique style for furniture, 61; carpentry overseen, 88
Sloan's City and Suburban Architecture, 16
Sloan's Constructive Architecture, 16
Smith, Hamilton, 73
Steiff Piano Company, 65

Tensas Parish, Louisiana, 14
Tile: floor for Longwood, 59
Tin: use on roof, 51
Treasury Department, United States Government, 73

Uncle Frederick (Nutt family servant), 25

Under-the-Hill, Natchez, Mississippi, 23
United States Hotel, 12
University of Louisville, Kentucky, 22

Ventreys Col.: mentioned in Sloan letter, 60
Vicksburg, Mississippi, 73
Villa France (ship), 56
Virginia: William Nutt emigrated to, 19

Walnut Street, Philadelphia, Pennsylvania, 60
Walters, Jacob, 52
Ward, James, Haller, 80
Ward, James, Williams, 80
Ward, Merritt Williams, 80
Ward, Robert Julian, 80
Watson, J. F., 57
Whitney, Eli: cotton gin, 22, 24
Whittington, Dr. Homer A., 83
Willetts, Peter, 18n
William Henry Hotel, 12
Williams, Julia Augusta (Mrs. Haller Nutt), 22
Williams: Julia Nutt's family, 61
Winter Quarters Plantation, Louisiana, 14, 16, 22, 23, 26n, 27n, 73
Wood: use of, 51
Woodville Road, Natchez, Mississippi, 26, 74

PICTURE CREDITS

Library of Congress for figures 1, 2, 3, 4, 5, 6, 7, 10, 11, 12 and 13.

Miss Laura Carpenter for illustrations used on pages 11, 15, 17, 32, 33, 34, 35, 45, 48, 49, 54, 55, 65, 66, 70, 71, 90, 91 and 95.

Miss Mildred McGehee for illustration used on page 30.

Historic American Buildings Survey for illustrations used on pages 37 and 44.

Miss Ann Aptaker for figure 7.

Duke University for figure 8.

Dr. Thomas Howard Gandy Collection for illustrations used on pages 89 and 93.

Mrs. D. R. Smith for illustration used on page 85.

Miss Mabel Lane for illustrations used on pages 20 and 21.

Printed in the USA
CPSIA information can be obtained
at www.ICGtesting.com
LVHW080835250824
788935LV00003B/35